HOW TO BECOME AN EMOTIONALLY-SAVVY ADULT

A Program in Leadership

JAN BOOTH, M.S.

authorHOUSE®

AuthorHouse™
1663 Liberty Drive
Bloomington, IN 47403
www.authorhouse.com
Phone: 833-262-8899

Published by AuthorHouse 01/19/2021

ISBN: 978-1-6655-0916-9 (sc)
ISBN: 978-1-6655-0915-2 (hc)
ISBN: 978-1-6655-0914-5 (e)

Library of Congress Control Number: 2020923891

Print information available on the last page.

CONTENTS

DEDICATION

This book is dedicated to my husband and family for exemplifying the principles included within these pages. It is also dedicated to anyone searching for a path to rise above current challenges or simply to enrich one's personal relationships. May these lessons and messages help you understand the worth of your soul and the amazing contributions you have within to bring peace and joy to our world.

ACKNOWLEDGEMENTS

I run a nonprofit organization that provides education to prison inmates in Utah. After meeting Jan Booth, she contacted me to offer her services. She developed and taught a course for prison students dealing with the critical relationship between thoughts and actions. It has become one of our most popular courses with Jan having worked individually with several dozen students in providing personalized, encouraging feedback to each. As I have read prisoner responses to Jan's personal encouragement, I found that she touched them at their core and provided hope.
Don Wright, Ph.D., President
PrisonEd Foundation

I have had the privilege and honor of knowing Jan Booth for over forty years. Seldom in my life have I ever met a more compassionate and genuinely caring person than Jan. Her love and light transcend all barriers the world would deem to place on us. She has devoted her life to the benefit of lifting and helping those in mental or emotional pain in whatever capacity is needed.
Jan is a brilliant author, listener, caregiver, and devoted friend to not only me, but everyone in my life. Jan's unique gifts touches hearts with her insightful words of wisdom and love.
Kathryn S. Peters

My husband and I have been friends with Jan for over forty years. I know that you are aware of how impeccable her credentials are but that is just a small part of what sets Jan apart. Despite the trials that Jan has experienced in life, she still manages to be the most positive person I know. She has the ability to turn lemons in her life to lemonade, truly a gift. A few years ago, one of my daughter's said it best, "You know, mom, if you want to feel good about yourself you just need to be around Jan for five minutes." If anyone can help youth find a way to beat and conquer their challenges, it is Jan Booth.
Debra Johnson

Jan Booth possesses an elevated ability to care for others on a personal level, and it shows in every aspect of her work. I have seen her make innumerable personal sacrifices to serve, uplift, and influence. She is a leader who actively seeks to bring out the best in others. Jan has a rare understanding of the emotional and psychological challenges that are faced by many but are rarely shown outwardly. She uses her knowledge and experience to empathize with those fighting inner battles and teaches them skills to help grow into their potential.

Demetrius Matuauto
Senior Revenue Accountant
Venafi Inc

I work for a non-profit organization in Utah that offers support and resources to juvenile offenders during and after incarceration. As a new organization, the need for obtaining a curriculum specific to Utah's juvenile population has been a top priority. I met Jan Booth after enrolling in two of her classes at Utah Valley University. She would often teach us concepts from her personal experiences working and serving for many years within Utah's prison walls. Jan has an in-depth knowledge of human nature, an aptitude for understanding the prison population, and an extraordinary ability to express herself. She also understands and designs curricula skillfully, particularly for inmate populations.

Shannon Pugmire, Group Facilitator - Second Chance 4 Youth

I am currently employed as a Certified Alcohol and Drug Counselor in Oregon. I have had the privilege of receiving instruction from Jan as an educator, friend, and colleague. My adolescent years were spent in turmoil as I struggled to process a number of traumatic events that I had experienced in my childhood. Incarceration, addiction, and destroyed relationships defined my young adulthood. Jan's magnificent ability to reach individuals like me was clear upon our first interaction. Without equivocation, I can attest to her unique ability to inspire others. Her course, "Becoming an Emotionally Savvy Adult: A Leadership Program for the Young Adult" offers a unique, groundbreaking curriculum designed to promote hope and facilitate change in young adults.

Ryan Gunderson
Certified Alcohol & Drug Counselor I - Qualified Mental Health Associate

Jan has a remarkable way of being able to reach students. As a student in undergraduate studies, I treasured each class I had an opportunity to take from her. She involves the students not only in theory but also in searching within themselves to find their own truths. She is an inspiring educator with an ability to bring out the absolute best in her students. She encourages self-discovery and for students to build upon theories that are already constructed and sound and find greater relevancy within them.

There are a handful of professors when you graduate that you remember, their lessons and their presence stay with you. Jan Booth is at the top of that list. It has been my boon to learn from her as a professor, my fortune to have her as a mentor, and a treasure to call her a friend. Rarely are such empathy, wisdom, and guidance given so freely.

James Crandall – Previous Student

I am a former student of Jan Booth. I took Personality Theory from her. I can remember thinking how dry the topic sounded by the class description, and I was pleasantly surprised after my first class with Jan. She is fun and has a lot of passion for all she does. Jan has also been a great help to me personally when I was struggling with my son who is on the autism spectrum. She has excellent insight and experience working with troubled youth.

Shannon Jewkes - Former Student

The youth and adult participant would be in very capable and loving hands with Jan. At her core she would care about them and provide important insight to help them pursue their dreams. She would always have their best interest at heart.

Lorie Lemmons

Gratitude
Gratitude lifts the spirit of the natural man or
woman to the heights of heaven.
My gratitude to my husband lives through the ages. His support is
unwavering, his guidance ever-present, and his love unconditional.

I thank my children and their spouses for their
unending patience, artwork, photography, and ideas
for personal and professional enhancement.

Acknowledgements

Many thanks go to Melissa Moss for her guidance, patience, and support of this project, to Burgess Owens for laying a foundation for a program for youth, to help them move forward rather than backwards. And, to Shannon Pugmire for her continued faith in me. To Kathryn Peters for her willingness to offer advice and photography, to Telisa Van Leuwen, Alex Booth, Laura Griffiths, Audrey Matuauto, and Emmie Montanez for their contributions of art and photography. I also thank Kelly Griffiths for financial advice, Tammie Booth and Joey Montanez for love and kindness, Ryan Gunderson for his belief in the program and my work, to James Crandall for friendship and courage, Shannon Jewkes for her many examples in perseverance, Gina Booth for offering very important knowledge on factors in educating youth, and Dave Booth for loving friendship. I thank Debra Johnson, and Lorie Lemmons for their support and ideas, and writing expertise and support of Dr. Don Wright. I acknowledge the great mentorship I have received from Dr. Cameron John, Dr. Bart Poulson, Dr. Brett Breton, and Dr. Ron Hammond of Utah Valley University, and computer specialist Shawn Edwards for always being willing to help. I thank Dr. Jeff Sheffield for guidance when the pathway to fruition for some of the lessons seemed ambiguous and he provided direction on how best to present the material. Buddy Dow has been incredible to work with. AuthorHouse is truly blessed to have him on their team. Rose Sheldon has offered important insights.

INTRODUCTION

I invite you into the world of someone very important, YOU! This is a journey, an opportunity for you to look within and find that amazing core of wonder that is you. Through life's challenges and personal choices, a person can get off-track and end up in serious situations thereby accumulating a series of bad habits that then control them. Self-defeating behaviors can alter the course of their lives. They may suffer consequences that sometimes take years to amend. For these reasons, this course is divided into 40 lessons/workshops. These personalized workshops will introduce you to positive tools for change through introspection, reflection, and study. I encourage you to dive into each assignment with full purpose of heart and to take from it what you need to make appropriate and positive changes in your life.

The New YOU – How thoughts affect your actions

You are strong, resilient, and important. You have much to offer yourself, family, peers, and those you are now, and will associate with in the future. Do you want that to be a positive influence or negative? It is up to you, not your circumstances. Wait, let me repeat that, it is up to YOU, not your circumstances. As you learn to think in a different, more optimistic way, you can embrace physical and emotional healing and wellness, compassion, and integrity. As you understand the power of taking responsibility for your life and actions, you invite honesty and understanding of others at a more profound level. These are keys for successful living.

This course embraces the concept of optimism. The converse of that is a state of hopelessness, but this can be changed to one of personal power and enlightenment. It takes effort, time, and commitment, but the reward far exceeds the effort! To begin with, allot yourself a specific time limit on any negative feelings such as hopelessness then start planning how to rise above your situation. What can you do to improve, truly improve, and change yourself internally?

Sit for just thirty seconds and tune into what you are feeling at this precise moment. After thirty seconds start flooding your mind with positive images, dreams, and goals for your future. Visualize your success, feel it, own it. Allow yourself to tune into those wonderful emotions of empowerment and hope. Make certain your desires are honorable and that they are worthy of a peacemaker and of an emotionally and spiritually strong individual. Do you want to improve your relationships with family, friends, and co-workers? Do you want to learn a skill or lesson? These lessons are designed for you to learn more about you and to take your experiences and knowledge and use it enrich the lives of others.

Write three things you can do now, meditate on these, and visualize them. Visit them several times a day in your mind. Keep your focus on the new you, the hopeful you, the improved you. This is a wonderful resource for you to refer to each day.

Consider the following statement.

Your perception is your reality.

What perceptions do you need to work on changing? If you grew up in poverty do you always need to be poor? If you grew up in a severely dysfunctional family, do you need to let that determine negative actions for your present or future relationships? Of course not! If you have an addiction is this going to determine your life from this moment on in a negative light or in a new view, one which embraces wisdom through learning from your addiction. Do you reinforce addictive and self-sabotaging thoughts and behaviors? If so, there is help for changing those to empowering and optimistic thoughts and successful aspirations. In essence, you have the strength and ability to climb out of your addiction or negative thinking mentality and to move in the direction of your positive dreams and goals.

What perceptions do you need to change? Many adults have that little child inside constantly replaying tapes that they are not good enough, they are not smart, and that they cannot change. All of that is erroneous and stunts their spiritual and emotional progression. Now is the time for change. This is the point in time for you to say, from this moment on, I choose to be a better, kinder, more honest person.

This course invites you into the world of great possibilities that can become realities if you but decide to make the commitment to read all the materials, ponder on them, pray if you are of the inclination, and let the journey of your new, healthy, responsible, compassionate, and honest self, begin. There are many true stories used for the lessons, followed by an activity. The more you put into each lesson the greater will be the benefit

Welcome to the course! –Jan Booth, M.S.

Course Objectives:

> ➢ Through reading and written work, students will identify areas of interest to them and relate them to the material offered.
> ➢ Students will offer opinions and personal insights on the meaning of the reading, citing specific quotes or comments and draw inferences from these to add to their responses and papers.
> ➢ Students will actively engage in the learning process by reading all material and completing each assignment.
> ➢ Students will develop a specific plan-of-action for becoming a role model and mentor for others.

Please take the following inventory before beginning the course.

Booth Self- Assessment Inventory

Instructions: Rate each item using a scale of
1 to 5 then answer the question.

**1 = Strongly Disagree, 2 = Disagree, 3 =
Neutral, 4 = Agree, 5 = Strongly Agree**

1. **I choose to be honest in my dealings.**

    1 Strongly Disagree 2 Disagree 3 Unsure 4 Agree 5 Strongly Agree

    What does this mean to you?

2. **I find it important to make sure my behaviors are in line with my beliefs.**

    1 Strongly Disagree 2 Disagree 3 Unsure 4 Agree 5 Strongly Agree

    Comments: Clarify your beliefs by completing the statements. Some ideas are being honest, loyal, dependable, kind, true to your word, moral, empathetic, having hope, helping others, etc.

    I believe in …

    I believe in …

    I believe in …

    I believe in …

    I believe in …

3. **In the past I followed the crowd, even if I knew what they were doing was wrong.**

   1 Strongly Disagree 2 Disagree 3 Unsure 4 Agree 5 Strongly Agree

   Describe your feelings now; looking back on the "previous" you, compared to the present, how have you changed you?

4. **I believe in myself.**

   1 Strongly Disagree 2 Disagree 3 Unsure 4 Agree 5 Strongly Agree

   Describe what believing in yourself means to you.

5. **I can accomplish my goals.**

   1 Strongly Disagree 2 Disagree 3 Unsure 4 Agree 5 Strongly Agree

   Describe what you believe you can accomplish.

6. **When I do not act in line with my beliefs, I feel remorse.**

   1 Strongly Disagree 2 Disagree 3 Unsure 4 Agree 5 Strongly Agree

   Provide an example of not acting in harmony with your beliefs.

7. **There are some people I believe have my bests interests in mind.**

   1 Strongly Disagree 2 Disagree 3 Unsure 4 Agree 5 Strongly Agree

   List these people and how they show you that they care and want you to experience success.

8. **There are ways I show that I am honest.**

   1 Strongly Disagree 2 Disagree 3 Unsure 4 Agree 5 Strongly Agree

   List three ways you exemplify integrity.

9. **I consider other's feelings when I say or plan to do something.**

   1 Strongly Disagree 2 Disagree 3 Unsure 4 Agree 5 Strongly Agree

   Comments: Explain with an example.

10. **I am resistant to change.**

    1   2   3   4   5   6   7   8   9   10

    Comments: Are you open to learning new ways of doing things and to use those ideas? Provide an example.

11. **No matter how hard I try I never succeed.**

    1 Strongly Disagree 2 Disagree 3 Unsure 4 Agree 5 Strongly Agree

    Provide an example of feeling that defeated or one of experiencing success.

12. **I am willing to do what it takes to change and make a better life for myself, a life without harming others.**

    1 Strongly Disagree 2 Disagree 3 Unsure 4 Agree 5 Strongly Agree

    What do you view as your biggest obstacle in changing?

13. **It is up to me to make a success of myself.**

    1 Strongly Disagree 2 Disagree 3 Unsure 4 Agree 5 Strongly Agree

    If you answered that you agree, when did you realize this?

14. **I am clear in my goals for what I want to accomplish in the next twelve months.**

    1 Strongly Disagree 2 Disagree 3 Unsure 4 Agree 5 Strongly Agree

What is your one-year goal?

15. I am clear in my goals for what I want to accomplish in the next five years.

1 Strongly Disagree 2 Disagree 3 Unsure 4 Agree 5 Strongly Agree

What are your five-year goals?

16. I would like to be trained as a youth mentor.

1 Strongly Disagree 2 Disagree 3 Unsure 4 Agree 5 Strongly Agree

Describe how you see yourself helping others.

17. I know where I would like to do an internship.

1 Strongly Disagree 2 Disagree 3 Unsure 4 Agree 5 Strongly Agree

Describe your desired internship.

18. Describe one to three areas you feel you could mentor youth.

Lesson 1

Does MY Life Matter?

How wonderful it is that nobody need wait a single moment
before starting to improve the world.
-Anne Frank

The Messenger of Optimism

The question "Does MY life matter" has been asked repeatedly since the inception of mankind. It is a multi-faceted question, yet one which demands that the seeker of truth view themselves beyond their personal physical appearance and attributes. The answer lies within the soul and lines the heart, ignites the brain, and broadens one's perspectives and horizons. Dr. Melanie Greenberg (2012) wrote, "The biggest struggle in life is to know, embrace, and accept ourselves, with all of our faults and imperfections."[1]

Each of us has strengths and each has weaknesses and challenges that are sometimes so daunting an individual may not feel they can overcome them. However, the good news is, every person can conquer their challenges if they learn to believe in themselves and know how to reach out for help. This is a program designed for you. It is an invitation to truly look within, see where you need to "fix" things, recognize the areas you need help with, and design plans for your future. It is a plan-of-action for you to visualize and actualize your successful self, a person who is not involved in self-sabotaging activities, but instead, one who is thriving in life and making a positive difference to themselves and others.

Consider the case of a young woman whose freedom was taken from her. She had done no wrong, but she and her family had to go into hiding because military personnel were looking for them simply because they were not the race the leader thought they should be. It was World War II and Hitler's power grew so great that his dogma that anyone who was not completely what he determined to be "the perfect race" was to be exterminated. Her name is Anne Frank, and this is her story, (Anne Frank from biography.com)[2]

Anne's family watched as friends were taken and killed or sent to concentration camps. Hitler was training his soldiers to massacre millions simply because they were different and undeserving of life or protection. Anne's parents recognized this and prepared a place of hiding. There Anne lived for a period of four years, but her love of family and mankind ruled over the hatred. Her kindness and desire to be a peacemaker overcame her fears, and through her writings we were given the gift of seeing the wisdom, courage, forgiveness, optimism, and peace in a young woman, still a child, who eventually had all things taken from her.

The years were 1942-1944, the height of World War II. Young Anne was of Jewish descent. The Nazis were after her family. Just because they were Jews the Nazis wanted to send them to concentration camps. The hatred engendered by Hitler and his regime sent terror throughout Europe and subsequently throughout the world. The Franks and so many others lived in fear. But Anne allows us to catch a glimpse of her world, through her adolescent eyes as she grapples with the sociological events of her world, as well as coming to understand her own life and the process of maturation, crushes, and the importance of friends.

How does this apply to you? What if you were sent to a concentration camp for being male, or female? For your race or religion? Or, what if the person you loved most in the world was taken away from you? Would you strike out in revenge or learn to cope in a manner that will lean into your own strengths and connect with your soulfulness?

When Anne was thirteen her mother gave her a great gift. It was not a cell phone or tablet. Those were not even invented at that time. Her mother loved Anne and was grateful to be able to give her this one present, a journal, which Anne named, Kitty. And remember, the family was in hiding. She was thirteen and wanted to be with her friends and talk about thirteen-year-old girl topics, perhaps boys she had a crush on or worries about friends and plans for the future, changes in her body, upcoming community parties, and school dances! Sadly, all of these were stolen from her because of hatred and fear. Instead, she lived in hiding and the daily threat of being found.

Anne was thrilled and poured onto paper the contents of her mind and heart. She could not call, text, or visit friends. She couldn't go outside the walls of the building in which she was hiding, but she could do one thing, <u>determine what her attitude would be</u>. Anne decided to find joy in her isolation and expression through her writings. Little did she know that for 75 years and continuing her journal would give hope to the downtrodden and light to the darkness within. She wrote in her diary from June 12, 1942 until August 1, 1944 when the Nazis took captive Anne and her family. In 1944, Gerri Bolkestein, who was a member of the Dutch government in exile, asked for people to share their thoughts, poems, and diaries to provide historical personal narratives of individuals affected by the war. Until her capture, Anne rewrote and edited parts, yet kept the original in-tact. Her father was able to keep it hidden until he published it. (Frank and Pesller, n.d.)[3]

One of her ambitions was to be a writer. Her mother certainly recognized this and gave her the gift to launch her talents into the desires of her heart. Her mother could not grant her physical freedom, but she could give her freedom of expression onto paper.

Anne and her family hid in a secret annex in a business building her father owned. For months, her parents had realized they would eventually need to hide. Many of their friends had already been sent to concentration camps simply for being Jewish so they had established this secret hiding placing in advance and were ready when they knew it was time to leave their home, leave their friends, and go into hiding. Anne's sixteen-year-old sister, Margot, had been "called up" which meant she had been ordered by the Nazi secret police, "The Gestapo" to be taken and placed in a concentration camp so the family immediately fled to the annex to hide for as long as possible. This move kept the family in-tact for two years. Then, on August 4, 1944, they were all arrested. Just a few months later, in January of 1945 Anne's mother died of hunger in Auschwitz and in February or March of 1945 Anne and her sister, Margot, died of typhus in the Bergen-Belsen concentration camp. Somehow their father survived and eventually published Anne's diary and other writings, History.com Editors (2020)[4].

Imagine the terror Anne and her family lived with. But Anne refused to give into fear and hopelessness. She wrote pages and pages of thoughts, feelings, fears, and joy. Throughout her diary the reader becomes witness to her moments of wonderful optimism, laughter, harmony, peace, and most of all love. This quote is so indicative of the character of this young woman:

> *Everyone has inside of him a piece of good news.*
> *The good news is that you don't know how great you can be!*
> *How much you can love! What you can accomplish!*
> *And what your potential is!*
> -Anne Frank (June 12, 1929-February/March 1945)

Anne Frank is an example of courage, determination, and faith. Though she was restricted in her life, and she witnessed the death of loved ones and fellow citizens, she still sought to bring hope to her family and to all she met.

Lesson

I invite you to take time to read each lesson, think about it, and delve into it at the visceral (gut level) emotional/spiritual level. As you think about the lesson, do the activities and exercises, and engage in discussion you will find great insights into YOU and YOUR life. I ask you to be honest in your writings and discussions. This program is, as I stated, for YOU! So, when you ask Does MY life matter you are looking at your purpose for being; why you are here on the earth at this time and in your own circumstances. Consider what you have in strengths that can contribute to society as a whole and to the individuals you meet on your pathway through life. Think about your skills and personality traits. How can you access those to lead others to have great hope for their future and faith in themselves? You do, indeed, matter.

The issues and topics we will be discussing include some of those provided below.

- ➢ Wouldn't it be great to know that YOU CAN transform emotions that have previously hijacked you into self-destructive behavior to feelings, thoughts and behaviors that will, instead, benefit you and others?
- ➢ How you can become more aware of yourself, your thoughts and emotions?
- ➢ Did you know that when you learn to take responsibility for your actions you can actually accomplish more and learn to serve others with truth and clarity?
- ➢ What if you could learn how to develop a greater sense of self-discipline and self-control? Think of the outstanding things you could accomplish!
- ➢ What about your boundaries? You will learn how to determine who you want in your personal space and how to release the toxic people from your life space.
- ➢ How would you like to learn how to positively direct your strengths and overcome those areas holding you back?

> ➤ Are you aware that you do have the power to forgive others? This is a tough subject, but you will learn how to do that and how to give others time to forgive you.
> ➤ You will learn to be emotionally aware of your own feelings and their importance and the emotions of others.
> ➤ The topic of those areas that are self-sabotaging will be discussed.
> ➤ You will learn to be a leader and mentor to others.

Activity

Does "MY Life Matter" is a question for each person to consider. We are more than a name, more than a gender, and more than a nationality. For this first lesson consider all dimensions of self by using the Holistic Health Model. This model includes five areas: physical, social, emotional, intellectual, and spiritual. Using this model, you are instructed to answer the following questions.

1. Why are you taking this course?
2. Write about you, where you grew up, describe your family life and how conflict was addressed and how love was shown.
3. Describe yourself physically in terms of your health and discuss how to improve this and include what more you can do to take better care of yourself.
4. Describe yourself socially by writing what this means to you and write how you can be a better friend to others.
5. Describe yourself emotionally and write how you can better care for yourself in this aspect and what that will mean for you in your future. This would include how you manage anger, how you perceive your present life and your emotions attached to that.
6. Describe yourself intellectually and tell what you can do to learn new and exciting things, get more schooling, and find what you want to do as a career.
7. Describe yourself spiritually by writing what spirituality means to you and if you think it is important, why or why not.

Footnotes

1   Greenberg, M. (2012, Oct 1). *The 50 Best Quotes on Self-Love.* Found online December 17, 2019 from https://www.psychologytoday.com/us/blog/the-mindful-self-express/201210/the-50-best-quotes-self-love

2   Anne Frank http://www.biography.com/people/anne-frank-9300892#nazi-occupation

3   Frank, O. & Pressler, M. (Eds). (n.d.) *The diary of a young girl: The definitive edition.* http://www.rhetorik.ch/Aktuell/16/02_13/frank_diary.pdf

4   History.Com Editors. (2020, Jul 1) *Anne frank.* https://www.history.com/topics/world-war-ii/annefrank-1

Lesson 2

Who AM I?

And you? When will you begin that long journey into yourself?
— **Rumi**

MY Own Journey to SELF

As you view your own struggles, your personality, dreams, and goals one thing to consider is the greatness you have within. However, sometimes that can be hidden by the challenges of life. This is a true story of a man who rose above adversity to embrace resiliency with courage, tenacity, and faith. His name is Roy Tasker[1] (Tasker, 2016).

Roy suffered severe abuse at the hands of his father. The reader of his book may wonder why the mother didn't step in and take care of Roy and his brothers, then as one reads further, they realize that his mother simply felt incapable of protecting him or his siblings.

Each day, Roy knew he would get beaten, physically and emotionally. His father repeated messages of what a failure he was, and he grew up feeling unloved, unimportant, and having no sense of worth. He did, however, have a kernel of faith within him that he could accomplish something if he put his mind to it. There were many roadblocks, one being a brain injury from his father's abuse, so learning was very difficult for him. Still, learning to read was his passion. He was placed in special education programs at school, but he simply could not read. His desire was so strong that when he was a young man, he taught himself to read and learn through listening to cassette tapes and practicing repeating what they said. He could follow along in a book if he chose to.

Roy dreamed of having a better life, he had internal motivation to stay strong, follow his dreams and not give up. When he was about sixteen, he left home. He was on his own, no one to turn to for help, but he was determined to make it on his own. At that point Roy was homeless, sleeping wherever he could, somehow surviving. Eventually he met a young woman and they married and had a family. Sadly, she left him. He took different jobs, so he could support his family, and continue moving forward.

Passions filled Roy's mind giving him direction in life. He loved being outside and enjoyed landscape work, so he started a landscaping business and was doing well with it! He was excited and wanted to share his success with his father, just hoping for recognition and praise. Here is an example of a man desperately seeking the approval of his father, which never came. Instead, he was ridiculed and told he would fail. Unfortunately, Roy bought into the messages and soon lost his truck to the bank and his business went under. His father's predictions came true because Roy internalized them and once again felt like a failure and that he would never succeed. This translated to his work, and he lost the business. Later, he realized that he had allowed his father's opinion to take root in his mind until he, too, believed he would fail. This is a very important point. Regardless of negative messages you may have received, it is up to you to dream big, make concrete plans for accomplishing pro-social and healthy goals that will benefit you, your family, and community, and to move forward on this. Sometimes this also means asking for help.

Roy was now a single parent, which was a challenge, as millions of people know. Roy was raising his children on his own, had lost his income, and was virtually at a hopeless point in life, a dangerously dark state of mind to be in. Suddenly, one of his children awakened from sleep and talked to his father. That little voice brought him to his senses, and he started to change his thoughts. This was a significant "spiritual" intervention that truly altered the course of his life.

Roy gathered his children, found a laundromat in town, and once again began to live with intent. When he entered the laundromat, a sweet elderly woman was there to welcome him. She told him to go wash the children and she would take care of his laundry. This was actually surprising to him that someone would care about him and his family. Her gentle kindness was something he had not experienced. When the children and laundry were clean, she sent them on their way, each of them feeling loved and cared for; Roy, re-energized at a more meaningful level, not only physically, but emotionally and spiritually, as well.

Periodically, Roy returned to the laundromat always at the same time of night and each visit proved to be just as inviting as the previous. The same woman was there. It was as if she was waiting for them. She greeted them with love and joy and immediately took over their laundry so he could care for his children. This little bit of encouragement was vitally important in Roy's story. Some may say she was an angel, others that the universe helped him, and some said that God stepped in. Regardless, there were definite miracles on Roy's journey. The first was his son simply awakening from sleep and talking to him, asking him what he was doing at a point he was wondering how he could go on. The other times included the woman at the laundromat giving each of his children and himself that genuine gift of positive support and compassion that ignited the hope within them all.

During the next few months Roy worked hard and began to experience success, internally and externally. He was living independently, could take care of his children, and was finally feeling stable. After a year had passed, he and his children returned to the laundromat. He wanted to thank the woman and show her that he was now doing well, that his children were provided for, and that her help had meant so much to him, to them all. He truly was thriving in business, and most importantly, as a father. Eagerly he approached the building but to his surprise she was not there. There was someone else working, and when he inquired about his friendly helper, the woman he spoke with had no knowledge of his "angel" friend, even after he described her in detail. She told him that no one of that description had ever worked at that location. Here is another interesting fact, when Roy told her the details of the dates and times, he and his family would frequent the laundromat this woman reported that she had worked there twenty years and the laundromat was never opened during those hours he claimed to have been there! It was then he realized that the elderly woman was somehow an "angel" sent to rescue him.

Roy believed in himself and through his words you can grasp the importance of that for continuing one's journey. "You are exactly where you need to be, and everything that you have experienced up to this point make you who you are today. So, be at peace with your current situation wherever you are." (Tasker, R. 2016. p. 102)[2]

Lesson

You are where you are now through many choices you have made. To be at peace with yourself means to accept your current situation and then determine what you can do this day to make your life better. What do you need to change within yourself? How can you help others? What matters is now and each new tomorrow. What does the future hold for you? That is, of course, your choice. Regardless of your circumstances, you have what it takes to live in harmony with the wonder that you have within. You are courageous and strong. This course is for you. It is an invitation to apply honest self-appraisal, fix what needs fixing, find help for those areas requiring added influence, and making the choice to be that person of great worth that lies within. You have specialized skills, and intrinsic drive to make a positive difference in a world that can, at times, be harsh and unforgiving.

Roy endured abuse and trauma. He was raised in an emotionally unsafe home and eventually had to grab hold of life to accomplish his dreams and in doing so release the negative messages he had grown up with. He taught himself to read. He determined to be the father and man he had not seen modeled for him. He committed his life to his family and to helping others. He used to believe he would fail, but his turning point came with the voice of his little child, the help of an "angel" and the core of faith. He is a man whose story is one of courage, determination, and hope.

Activity

1. Review Roy's story and write down the parts that affected you the most and why.
2. List three strengths you have in overcoming challenges.
3. Discuss three pieces of advice you would offer to another person going through challenges.

Footnotes

1   Tasker, Roy. (2016). Upside Down & Backwards with the Law of Attraction. Avatar Publications, Inc.
2   Ibid.

Lesson 3

Dimensions of Personality

Positive expectations are the mark of the superior personality.
-Brian Tracy

What is Personality?

The study of self is a personal research project into learning more about yourself, your emotions, how they affect your life, your temperament, interests, goals, and beliefs. First, we address the issue of personality, which is very complex. The psychology dictionary defines it as:

> "The configuration of personality traits and actions which includes a person's individual acclimation to life, inclusive of primary traits, interests, motivations, morals, self-concept, skills, and emotional trends. Character is usually seen as a complicated, dynamic consolidation or entirety, formed by multiple forces, inclusive of: genetic and constitutional propensities, physical growth- formative training-identification with important people and groups- socially

conditioned morals and roles- and vital experiences and unions." (https://psychologydictionary.org/personality/)

That is a lot of explanation for saying what Webster wrote so well, "…The quality or state of being a <u>person</u>…the complex of characteristics that distinguishes an individual or a nation or group *especially*: the totality of an individual's behavioral and emotional characteristics." https://www.merriam-webster.com/dictionary/personality.

An online search into words meaning the same as personality, brought up the following indicators: charisma, charm, identity, makeup, nature, psyche, self, temper, temperament, complexion, disposition, dynamism, emotions, individuality, magnetism, singularity, likableness, selfdom, selfhood. (https://www.thesaurus.com/browse/personality)

The point being that we are each complex, we have our own histories and belief systems, our own ways of learning and behaving. This course is designed to teach you more about yourself and others and to provide tools for living which will assist you throughout your life.

Lesson

The OCEAN inventory is a personality assessment looking specifically at five areas of life, OCEAN meaning Openness to Experience. Conscientiousness. Extraversion. Agreeableness. Neuroticism. Of course, we each have a combination of these, and there is not one specific personality inventory that can cover all aspects of a person's complexities. Provided below is a review of the five areas. Remember, we each have a combination of these.

Activity

1. Read the different categories and underline those traits <u>you feel you have</u>.
2. Circle the traits <u>you would like to work on</u> to develop.
3. Discuss as a class.

Open to Experience

John & Srivastava, (1999) [1] stated that openness to experience is the depth and complexity of a person's life and their experiences. They show a love for learning and digging into their areas of interest. They use imagination, creativity, and the ability to view things through a wide lens. The following lists of traits are provided by Ackerman (2019).[2]

Imagination	Insightfulness
Interested in different things	Originality
Daring	Likes variety
Cleverness	Creativity is engaging
Curiosity	Perceptiveness
Intellect	Complexity/Depth

Conscientious

This is the inclination to show self-restraint and choose to act in socially acceptable behaviors. People who are conscientious have goals and follow through on their plans They are able to delay gratification or reward, incorporate organizational effectiveness, and understand the process in working towards personal goals.

Persistent	Ambition
Follow-through on assignments/work	Self-discipline
Consistent	Predictability
Self-Control	Reliability
Find solutions, are resourceful	Hard work
Energetic	Persevere
Plan and set goals	

Extroversion

Extroversion invites a view from a double lens: extroversion and introversion. The extrovert is a person who recharges their personal "energy" batteries through interacting with others. Introverts replenish their personal energy and drive through seclusion, sometimes choosing to isolate for a short to a longer period of time. They take time to ponder and contemplate ideas and decisions while the extrovert is out-going, often even the very "life of the party" and may be quick to make decisions.

Sociable

Positive energy	Outgoing nature
Enjoys being around others	Talkative
Fun-loving nature	Self-Confident
Tendency for affection	Friendliness

Agreeable

The agreeable person gets along well with others. Those individuals high in agreeableness are generally popular, trusted, respected, and in tune with the needs of others. (Lebowitz, 2016a)[3]. Conversely, those low in agreeableness are not as likely to be respected and trusted; they can be brutally blunt, irritable and quick-to-outrage, hostile and sarcastic (Ackerman, 2019)[4].

Empathetic	Look for good in others
Modest	Humble, Willing to learn
Patient	Moderate, not extreme
Tactful and kind	Polite
Loyal	Sensitive
Unselfishness	Helpfulness
Cheerful	Considerate

Neuroticism

The characteristic of Neuroticism looks at an individual's level of self-competence and their own degree of comfort with themselves. In some cases, neuroticism can indicate a lower self-esteem and feeling of powerlessness and hopelessness. If a person is unsure of themselves and their abilities, it often shows up in their work and study habits. They may feel that their work really doesn't matter. When one feels unstable and vulnerable, it is difficult to work with a high level of competency. A 45-year study by Sodz and Vaillant (1999)[5] reported that a high level of neuroticism is correlated with a few more issues of addiction, depression, and other health issues. The key is to engage in behaviors and to learn new ways of thinking about things and viewing one's life. A person leaning towards this category is not locked into these traits, some have some and others not. Tools for healthy coping and self-efficacy development would be very beneficial and help the person lower their fears, anxieties, and feelings of inadequacy. It is important to realize the past is behind you and you can learn from it, release it and move forward. You are amazing. You are strong. You are able to build a healthy and peaceful, successful and happy life.

Footnotes

1   John, O. P., & Srivastava, S. (1999). The Big-Five trait taxonomy: History, measurement, and theoretical perspectives. In L. A. Pervin & O. P. John (Eds.), *Handbook of Personality: Theory and Research* (Vol. 2, pp. 102-138). New York: Guilford Press.

2   Ackerman, C. E. (2019, November 7). Big five personality traits: The OCEAN model explained. Retrieved 17 December 2019 from https://positivepsychology.com/big-five-personality-theory/

3   Lebowitz, S. (2016a). The 'Big 5' personality traits could predict who will and won't become a leader. *Business Insider*. Retrieved from http://www.businessinsider.com/big-five-personality-traits-predict-leadership-2016-12

4   Ackerman, C. E. (2019). November 7). Big five personality traits: The OCEAN model explained. Retrieved 17 December 2019 from https://positivepsychology.com/big-five-personality-theory/

5   Soldz, S., & Vaillant, G. E. (1999). The Big Five personality traits and the life course: A 45-year longitudinal study. *Journal of Research in Personality, 33,* 208-232. doi:10.1006/jrpe.1999.2243

***Using the Internet, an online self-scoring Five-Factor (OCEAN) personality test can be taken. It can be found at https://www.psychometrictest.org.uk/big-five-personality/

Lesson 4

Excitement and Value in Learning

THINK

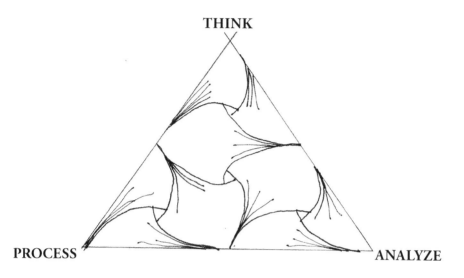

PROCESS

ANALYZE

Character is doing the right when when nobody's looking.
There are too many people who think that the only thing that's right
is to get by, and the only thing that's wrong is to get caught.
-J.C. Watts

Learning to Learn

Why is learning how to learn important? Consider the most exciting movie you have seen. What were the details, why was it important to you? Did it teach anything? Who's your favorite hero? What have you learned about him/her? Bhasin (2019) wrote that "…learning is an indispensable tool that nourishes our minds and soothes our soul. It is a necessity for both personal and professional career as it makes us capable of understanding and handling things in a better way. "[1] Learning helps with understanding critical thinking, how to analyze and synthesize information. It is the ability to think through things, to learn to make better decisions.

Benjamin Bloom, an educational psychologist presented a taxonomy for learning. His desire was to increase critical thinking skills so greater depth in learning could occur. Why is this important and how is it relevant to relationships? In the last module we discussed hidden emotions with the umbrella analogy. Today, I am showing you the Bloom's Taxonomy vs. the newer one presented by Lorin Anderson and David Krathwohl. ProEdit(2013)[1]

Dr. Bloom organized a group to decide upon specific steps to mastering concepts or ideas and from there designed Bloom's Taxonomy. In the 1990s, Lorin Anderson and David Krathwohl expanded the taxonomy to be more active and personally adaptable by including "create" as the highest category in the taxonomy. (ProEdit.com, 2020)[2]

Lesson

How often have you taken a class and failed to see its relevancy? What about having trouble retaining the information? When the topic is meaningful to you your level of commitment to listening and learning increases. Consider the following questions. Your attitude makes a difference, **the** difference.

1. I came into the course having low expectations.　T　F
2. I came into this course with a positive attitude.　T　F
3. I am interested in becoming a mentor.　T　F
4. I am willing to complete the work to become a mentor.　T　F
5. I am committed to setting positive, achievable goals.　T　F
6. I am interested in getting an internship.　T　F
7. I am willing to ask for help when I need it.　T　F

Activities

1. Review the two different taxonomies. They are very similar, but the newer version invites the ability to be creative, which means you create something new. It could be a new solution to an

on-going problem. It could be a work of art to depict your mood. Anything is possible.

2. Using the bottom chart dissect one problem you are facing. Using the new taxonomy devise a plan of action for handling the situation. The taxonomy goes from the bottom to the top, but for the purposes of this activity the order is reversed.

3. Discuss with the instructor and/or the class.

Traditional Model	**Revised Model**
Benjamin Bloom's Original Taxonomy (1956)	**Lorin Anderson's and David Krathwohl's Change to Taxonomy (2000)**
Top Level of Taxonomy Evaluation Can the learner analyze and judge the information to determine if it is noteworthy or if it needs to be altered, are they able to rationally critique it?	**Top Level of Taxonomy Creating** Can the learner actually use the information to write, speak, or create something that is new from the information provided?
↑ Synthesis ↑ Can the learner analyze the information to determine if it is noteworthy or if it needs to be altered to create something new or different?	↑ Evaluating ↑ Can the learner analyze the information to determine if it is noteworthy or if it needs to be altered, critique it?
↑ Analysis ↑ Can the learner dissect the information, categorize it and see how it is important or memorable?	↑ Analyzing ↑ Can the learner dissect the information, categorize it and see how it is important or memorable?
↑ Application ↑ Can the learner apply what they have learned, make it relevant and useful?	↑ Applying ↑ Can the learner apply what they have learned, make it relevant and useful?
↑ Comprehension ↑ Does the learner understand the lesson or information provided?	↑ Understanding ↑ Does the learner comprehend the lesson or information provided?

↑ Knowledge ↑	↑ Remembering ↑
The ability to learn and retain information.	The ability to learn and retain information

Personalized Model

New Taxonomy Model	YOUR Ideas
REMEMBERING What is the problem?	
UNDERSTANDING What is YOUR understanding of the issue?	
APPLYING How can you apply your skills and knowledge to this situation?	
ANALYZING What is your analysis of why the problem exists and what does it mean to you in your life and current circumstances?	
EVALUATING Dissect your problem. Think of things you or others may not have understood. How can you view things differently?	
CREATING What is your game plan for solving this problem or issue? What can you do today to begin this process?	

Footnotes

1   Bhasin, H. (2019, December 2). What is the importance of learning (In any stage of life). https://www.marketing91.com/importance-of-learning/

2   ProEdit.com. (2020). Understanding Bloom's (and Anderson and Krathwohl's taxonomy. Retrieved from https://www.proedit.comunderstanding-blooms-and-anderson-and-krathwohls-taxonomy.

Lesson 5

Embracing YOUR Future: Designing YOUR Personal GPS

*Our success at friendship, business, sports, love –
indeed, at nearly every enterprise we attempt –
it is largely determined by our self-image.
People who have confidence in their personal worth
seem to be magnets for success and happiness.*
-Alan Loy McGinnis

The Boy and a Drum

A Hindu legend tells the story of a little boy who really wanted a drum[1]. His parents were very poor and could not afford one, but she gave him a stick to play with. He wondered why she would give him a simple stick but, as little boys do, used his imagination and went off to play. Suddenly he sees an elderly woman who struggling to light her stove, what she called a chulha. The boy was excited, "I can help," he told her and gave her his stick. She was so grateful, and they talked for a while. She made bread, oh that bread smelled so delicious then she gave him half a loaf of bread! Joyfully he continues on his path and hears the crying of an infant. A potter's wife was desperately seeking food, she had none to give her child.

The little boy happily gave her the bread. The woman was so grateful that she gave him one of her pots. Now this little boy thought of things he could put in the pot, still not sure what to do with it. He came upon a river and a husband and wife were arguing. The boy listened and realized the husband was angry because the woman had broken the only pot they had. He gave them his pot, turned to leave and they gave him a coat. He wasn't cold, but graciously accepted the coat. Soon he found a bridge, then saw a small, weak man shivering, and he quickly ran over and gave him the coat. The man told the little boy he had been robbed, everything stolen from him but his horse and that he was very grateful for the coat. The man gave the boy his horse. The little boy walked the horse into town and heard lots of music and laughter. There was a wedding party going on and he got to see the bright colors but when he looked closer, the entire family was sitting under a tree, moping and sad. Legend dictated that the bridegroom needed to ride into town on a horse to lead the procession, but he had no horse. "Take my horse," says the boy. The families were thrilled. The bridegroom asked the little boy what he could give him in return. The little boy saw all the drums surrounding the drummer, his eyes lit up and asked for one small drum. The musician happily gave it to him.

Lesson

This is an important story about getting out of oneself and allowing life to unfold. Often, things happen that we might interpret as frustrating or defeating but inviting a feeling of calmness and patience actually sets in motion other events, especially if one is generous and selfless like the little boy. Each step of his journey involved giving away the one item he carried with him and in the end, he got what he had asked for in the first place. Oftentimes the gifts we receive may be of a more abstract nature. We might get understanding from another, learn wisdom, have a new appreciation of joy and gratitude. When we allow things to be replaced by soulful and compassionate living, we invite gifts of mercy or wisdom to eventually show up in our lives, and healings to occur. This is a way to embrace the future with confidence and renewed hope.

The picture at the top of this chapter is an aviator's Garmin GPS system. GPS means global positioning system. It shows the pilot where they are in a three-dimensional space giving latitude and longitude and altitude with a great degree of accuracy. It is also used for navigating the course to follow to get to the desired location. It allows shows terrain, so the pilot knows altitudes with different mountain ranges and an alert will sound within 1,000 feet of the terrain, including a mountain or heading towards rising terrain about ¼ of a mile away.

How does this interpret for YOU? You are in charge of your life. You set the parameters and others will try to pull you off course. In talking with one previous gang member serving time in prison his comment was that he was tired of giving into others and the gang life, tired of addiction, finally ready to do what he needed to for a better life.

Activity

1. Design your own GPS for your life. Use circles and instruments as shown here but instead of altitude and terrain write in those areas that will cause you to "crash and burn."
2. Include the ultimate destination of where you want to be in the next one to two years.

Footnote

1   Sharma, S. (17 November, 2017). The boy and the drum. *Bedtime short stories*. Retrieved from https://www.bedtimeshortstories.com/the-boy-and-the-drum

Lesson 6

What It Means to be Emotionally Savvy

Self-absorption in all its forms kills empathy, let alone compassion.
When we focus on ourselves, our world contracts
as our problems and preoccupations loom large.
But when we focus on other others, our world expands.
Our own problems drift to the periphery of the mind
and so seem smaller and increase our capacity for connection
– or compassionate action.
-Daniel Goleman

The Paradigm Shift

Stephen was a successful businessman. He was riding the subway in New York City. People were quiet, some reading, others just resting. It was a calm and relaxed setting. Suddenly a father with several children boarded the car he was in. The father sat next to him, seemingly oblivious to the fact that his children were running, throwing things, and disrupting everyone.

Finally, Stephen asked the man if he could calm his children, they were disturbing a lot of people. The father was surprised, seemed to come back to the present moment, and softly apologized. His wife had just died. The children had lost their mother and he simply did not know what to do. He hadn't even tuned into the chaos his children were causing. This was a game-changer for Stephen. He mentally stepped into the father's shoes and felt profound sadness for him and the children, then he turned to the grieving father and asked how he could help, Covey (2004)[1].

This is called a paradigm shift. It is when you suddenly have a new awareness and with that realize a profound opportunity for personal growth. This is what emotional intelligence is about. It is the ability to tune into your own feelings and those of others. It includes empathy and is about exercising self-control and finding new levels of awareness and patience. And it is a chance to consider the role of emotion as a major component of intelligence. How did it come about in such a profound way?

Another paradigm shift occurred when two psychology professors were painting a house and enjoying a discussion on politics. The men were John Mayer who became a professor at the University of New Hampshire, and Peter Salovey who moved onto be named as President of Yale University. They discussed education and the research they had conducted on emotions and cognitions, i.e., feelings and thoughts. They discussed someone on the world stage and asked how anyone who was known to be very intelligent had done something so stupid. Suddenly they concluded that "...smart decision-making requires more than the intellect as measured by traditional IQ", (Freedman, 2005)"[2].

This incident sparked their interest in the field of emotion vs. intellect in making decisions. They went on to publish an article on the topic in an obscure journal, but when Dr. Daniel Goleman, a psychologist, read the article his brain lit up and he grasped the importance of the message, so he started researching it and writing about it. His book, *Emotional Intelligence,* sold over 5 million copies and was printed in 30 different languages. They started a NexusEQ conference, EQ meaning emotional quotient and it became an international movement. Emotional intelligence looks at much more than IQ or intelligence. It takes into consideration emotions, interactions, communication, and thought processes.

Lesson

Freedman (2005) presented Goleman four-factors for emotional intelligence.[2]

> ➢ Self-awareness
> ➢ Self-management
> ➢ Social awareness
> ➢ Relationship management

In reviewing these four areas consider the following:

Self = Recognition and awareness of self: one's personal passion, their purpose in their life, family, work, education, knowledge of one's strengths and limitations, and an understanding of one's feelings.

Social = Having genuine consideration of others, empathy, healthy relationships, and inner leadership skills.

Self-Supervision = The ability to regulate and modulate moods, having self-restraint and discipline, and being willing to seek to learn and adapt to new situations.

Relationship-Management = Conversations that bring people together and handle conflict responsibly. There is the recognition of the importance in seeking more information, and transfer that knowledge to others, team building and organizing alliances within the family, team, business, and/or community[4].

Reading Other's Body Language- What is the person telling you without saying it?

- Self Centering:
  - o You are open to listening with ears, heart, mind, spirit, and eyes.

o You are aware of your own emotions and body positioning.
o "Open Yourself"- un-crossed arms, leaning forward to listen, and nodding along as you listen
• Body language indicators coming from the other person:
o Recognize if the other person can regulate their emotions via their actions.
o Maintain eye contact and read into face expressions.
o Recognizing positive signs of body language like
o Looking away or downward can be an indicator of shame, disagreement, fear, boredom, or anger
o Body tense, legs shaking or bouncing can be an indicator of nervousness

Emotional intelligence is important in personal and professional relationships. When a person has these characteristics, they create climates of trust, they invite honesty and compassion, they encourage people to try new things and, in this, they see that creativity can flourish. When a person feels at peace and safe, they can accomplish more difficult tasks and remain "in-tact" as a person. They feel invigorated rather than drained because they understand their work and commitment are valued.

Activities

1. Below is a list of characteristics of the emotionally savvy adult.
2. Circle which characteristics you would like to have and write what they mean to you.
3. Underline those characteristics you feel you have.
4. Discuss as a class. This activity allows you a more insightful glimpse into your own self-awareness.

Adaptable	Assertive, not Aggressive	Ability to Calm Self
Awareness of Emotions,	Awareness of Thoughts	Benevolent
Compassionate	Disciplined	Empathetic
Ability to forgive self	Ability to forgive others	Generous
Healthy Boundaries	Integrity-Based	Judicious
Kind	Listening Skills Refined	Loving and Lovable

| Optimistic | Open to New Experiences | Trustworthy |
| Responsible | Analyzes situations | Stops and thinks |

Footnotes

1   Covey, S. (2004). The 7 habits of highly effective people: Powerful lessons in personal change. NY: Simon & Schuster.
2   Freedman, J. (2005, Jan 30). Dr. Daniel Goleman on the origins of emotional intelligence. Six seconds.
3   Craig, H. (2019, Jan 8). 17 Emotional intelligence tests and assessments. Positivepsychology.com. Retrieved from https://positivepsychology.com/emotional-intelligence-tests/
4   Ibid.

Lesson 7

The Cobra Effect - Decisions and Consequences

Life presents many choices, the choices we make determine our future.
– **Catherine Pulsifer**

Beware of the Cobra

What a great title, "The Cobra Effect!" It invites speculation and visualization with its interesting history. The title was given during the years when England ruled over India. At that time there were too many cobras, very deadly snakes who were killing animals and people, so the government offered a bounty for any cobra killed. Soon, there were very few cobras left so those with an entrepreneurial spirit raised them, killed them, and turned them in for the bounty. When the government realized what was happening, they terminated the bounty on cobras, the result was that the cobras multiplied, and they were back to the original problem.[1]

This term, The Cobra Effect, occurs when there are unintended consequences or reactions to something such as that which had occurred in India. Another example is Airbus, who wanted their planes to be quiet, extremely quiet and peaceful, but an unintended effect occurred, everyone could hear noises within the plane, even anyone in the bathroom. A funny example, but one showing that a person or business can start out with a good motive, but have it result in unforeseen negative outcomes. How can one present a solution without a backlash adapting to this label of cobra effect?

A sad example of this is a young actor, Leif Garrett, who was successful as a teenage idol. However, his managers with ill-intent put such pressure on him that he became heavily involved in drugs and alcohol. Addictions ruled his life, his "voice" was taken from him and he became a pawn to the industry. He was the "poster child image" to bring in millions of fans to line the pockets of those who "owned" him. If we go back in time we see his mother recognizing his talent and trusting in the producer who stated he would treat him as his own son, when in reality he was the "wolf in sheep's clothing," taking advantage of the mother and son, and putting the son's life in jeopardy. The father was not involved with the boy and now the boy who is the man still yearns for the loving connection of his father and he is still coping with addiction, from the sober end of things. A seemingly positive choice to let the boy pursue his dream of acting turned everything completely around. He was promoted as a singer, his producer used him for money and power, greed took over, the boy was thrust into the world of drugs and sex and his life was put into shambles.

He stated, "For starters, when I was a teen idol, my managers would lie and say I was sick from exhaustion when, in reality, they wanted to make sure my shows were sold-out. So here I was, pretending to be sick, living this lie, just so that I can embody this perfect image of what they wanted me to be. It was wrong[2]."

Using one's intellect and tuning into feelings for direction is vitally important to succeed. In Mr. Garrett's situation his choice was stolen from him, now, as he has gained control over his life, he offers a new and healthier perspective. This is the choice you have, to look back on your life, see the good and recognize the problems and then choose from here to move forward with your dreams and goals.

Lesson

To succeed is an individualized decision, it is YOUR choice. Some choose to be successful in crime, others in humanitarian work, school, or a chosen profession, but the bottom line for true success in life is to realize two factors. It is up to the individual and it has a foundation of goodness. Each of us know of billionaires and multi-millionaires who employ a lot of people and make a lot of money. Much of what they do is good, some may be shady. The leader who stands above all is one who chooses kindness and mercy, hard work, integrity, faith, and benevolence. They cherish family. They honor relationships. They are honest in their dealings, and they are trustworthy. In an interview of Thich Nhat Hanh the interviewer asked if he was always calm and he replied that he had chosen that for himself since he was a boy. He had observed others, followed the intuitions and promptings of his "spiritual" self and chosen to be a leader for peace. He lives a life of gratitude and one seeking to bring peace to others.

How does this interpret for you? There is the "three strikes you are out" law in regard to criminals, but what if I offer you an alternative view? No more strikes, instead YOU choose to make amends, if it is the right thing to do, and change. Or, the other choice would be to step onto the ultimate Ferris wheel of criminal behavior and become the proverbial hamster on the wheel, repeating behaviors and mistakes, even crimes, and ending up in and out of jail and eventually, prison. We can see that one may steal to help someone else but in the long run, it hurts the person and others. Instead, one can seek help, work, and be responsible, take classes, follow their dreams, and become pro-social, active and successful members of society. YOU have the power to promote the success effect and negate the cobra effect.

Linking into the psychological and emotional well-being is an important step in overcoming current problems, negative thinking, and in learning new ways of coping and planning for the future.

Activities

1. Study the chart below and fill in your comments.[3]
2. As a class add two new strengths and challenges at the end.

Psychological and Emotional Stamina and Well-Being

Psychological/ Emotional Strengths	Psychological/ Emotional Challenges	Comments
I am able to cope well during challenging times.	I have difficulty coping when times are hard.	
I am able to keep my perspective during difficult times.	I lose my perspective in difficult times and resort to self-sabotaging behaviors	
I have an optimistic attitude in working through problems.	I tend to be negative during hard times.	
I have a sense of humor and can laugh at myself.	I don't see humor in things.	
I am good at solving problems.	It is hard for me to calm down to find a logical solution to a problem.	
I am independent, yet know who to turn to for help, if needed.	I am very dependent on others.	
I am able to ask for help.	I am independent to a degree but don't know where to turn for help.	
Add your own		
Add your own		

Footnotes

1   Davis, A. & Harrigan, J. R. (6 September, 2019). The Cobra Effect: Lessons in Unintended Consequences. Foundation for Economic Education. Retrieved from https://fee.org/articles/the-cobra-effect-lessons-in-unintended-consequences/

2   Nolasco, S. (4 January 2020). Former teen idol Leif Garrett explains descent into hard drugs: 'There has always been more to my story.' *Fox News.* Retrieved from
https://www.foxnews.com/entertainment/leif-garrett-teen-idol-memoir

3   Bozic, N., Lawthom, R., and Murray, J. (2018), Exploring the context of strengths – a new approach to strength-based assessment. *Educational Psychology in Practice.* Vol 34 No.

Lesson 8

I AM the Driver -
Knowing When It's Time to Change Directions

Incredible change happens in your life when you
decide to take control of what you do have power over
instead of craving control over what you don't.
— **Steve Maraboli, <u>Life, the Truth, and Being Free</u>**

Anton

Anton immigrated to the United States. He'd been born and raised in a home of poverty. Violence was the norm. His family came seeking a new way of life. They were concerned for his son, but his son was used to violence, continued to break the law and was arrested several times, finally resulting in a prison term. It was there that a handful of community volunteers helped him turn his life around.

Initially Anton was angry, rebellious, and continued fighting in prison. Finally, he began to listen to the concern people had for him and the pathway to peace and success they offered. He enrolled in classes and started to make specific plans for his future, one outside the walls of prison. Life isn't easy behind locked doors and Anton slipped back into old patterns, but a tiny intervention happened.

It was a time when Anton was at his lowest point. He simply didn't believe in himself any longer. One day he was sitting in the classroom waiting for the lesson to begin. His mind, however, was not on the lesson but an altercation with someone. In the past he would have engaged in a brutal fight, but he was tired or living in prison, and angry with one particular inmate. Still, he had a degree of self-restrain. One volunteer saw him sitting alone, she felt his sadness and went to sit beside him. They began talking and eventually the class started, and the conversation ended. Nothing of substance pertaining to his state of mind was provided the volunteer and she just went about her work. Six weeks later he sought her out, respectfully asking if he could speak with her for a moment. He then told her that on the day she had sat by him to talk he was on the verge of going after another inmate. The only factor that seemed to stop him was when he realized that she genuinely cared about him and saw him as a human being, not an inmate or someone who was disgusting. Those few moments provided the turning point for Anton and he expressed tremendous gratitude to her. He then went about his work, followed through on his plans for the future outside the prison, and determined what he needed to do to earn parole. He even offered a peaceful solution to the inmate he had previously been having problems with.

When Anton was young, there were not a lot of positive things happening in his life. For any child, each stage of development is important for learning tools for living. For the 12 to 17-year-olds it is a season of physical maturation and emotional identity seeking. It is a critical developmental stage in the life of a young man or woman and peer pressure can be intense. Anton had made poor choices in adolescence that carried on in adulthood. He was close to a few family members. but community influence was sketchy. Protective factors are gifts of kindness and honor that each of us needs throughout our lives. Anton finally came to realize that there were those who did care, and that if he resorted to previous behaviors, he would lose that positive edge to move forward in life and see a future of freedom.

The critical juncture came for Anton when he was debating on a violent act, which could have resulted in a life sentence, or he could use the skills he'd been taught over the past few years. He made the right choice.

and it changed his life. You have the opportunity today to expedite your commitment to personal excellence

Lesson

Life and people can intersect in different ways to offer each of us a helping hand. If you pay close attention to this short narrative of Anton's life, it is important to note those factors that helped him turn towards his dreams rather than remain stuck in the negative, crime-infested lifestyle he was familiar with. He could have resorted to violence and had a much different life.

What made the difference to him? I remind you of the term, "protective factors" which means that each person needs to have other people along their road in life to lend them a helping hand. Within the prison setting Anton had several people encouraging his success each with the message that he was able to do better than what he was doing. He experienced a personal crisis with identity confusion and had to step outside that negative circle of influence to open his mind to a better future. Ultimately, he realized, it was HIS decision, no one else's. Would he further succumb to the criminal life or follow his dreams? Instead of listening to the negative messages he started to tune into his inner voice. He set an academic and career plan and from that point on walked the pathway of making proactive decisions that would empower him through his life's dreams and goals. He moved from being a victim of his circumstances to becoming a man focused on success.

Activity

1. Draw a large steering wheel.
2. On the outside edge quickly write the initials of people who have had an influence on you in your entire life. Their influence could be positive or negative. You will have 60 seconds to do this.
3. Now, go back and give each set of initials a + or − sign to indicate who had a positive influence and who had a negative one. Some will actually have both signs.

4. Next, draw a smaller circle within the larger one.

5. Write the initials of anyone from the larger circle you still want to have in your life.

6. Draw a smaller circle in the center and write your name in the middle.

7. Write the initials of only those people you want closest to you; those you can truly share with.

8. Read the quote at the top of the page. Now write what that means to you.

9. As a class discuss how you can have more control in your life.

You are the master of your life, at various times and places
people will step in to help you over one more hurdle.
The key is to recognize those who want to help
and humbly allow them to do so.
Jan Booth

Lesson 9

"THINK," A Model for Emotion Mastery

(Sketch Courtesy of S. C. Booth)

Service is the bottom line to happiness and fulfillment.
Gail Halvorsen

The Pilot with Candy

It was the end of WWII. The Nazis had surrendered in 1945 and Adolf Hitler's regime had fallen but Joseph Stalin was ruling over the Soviet Union. Berlin was in the throes of poor economic conditions, and hopelessness. The western half of Germany was freed, having been rescued by the Americans, French, and British military. The eastern half remained under Communist control. Then, on June 24, 1948 Stalin ordered that any access to food, medicine, and coal was denied to over two million German citizens. The U.S. Air Force had only been formed nine months before. They were ordered to keep Berliners alive, and to prevent the Cold War from moving into another world war. It was a crucial time in history to maintain peace.

The Air Force were ordered to deliver food to the Western Berliners. The movement was labeled the Berlin Airlift and commenced on June 26, 1948. U.S. Air Force C-47 Skytrains along with C-54 Skymasters began to deliver flour, milk, and medicine to West Berlin. Over 2.3 million tons of supplies were delivered by the U.S. and British aircraft. Imagine watching this! Every three minutes aircraft landed bringing in 13,000 tons of food, medicine, coal, relief to the Western Berlin citizens.

1st Lt. Gail Halvorsen was one of the pilots, completing over 126 missions to deliver food and supplies from July of 1948 to February of 1949. The Air Force recognized Stalin as the new enemy, quickly and powerfully replacing Hitler. Even though months earlier the United States had been bombing Germany to stop the Nazi movement and win the war against Germany, now, they were feeding the people. What a heart-centered service this was, (Candy Bomber Delivered Chocolate, Hope to Berlin, 2018).[1]

The people of West Berlin were tired, hungry, and most of all, hopeless. They needed something to hold onto, something to cling to that their future would be better. Lt. Halvorsen loved taking pictures and movies and one day he noticed about 30 little German children standing outside watching the planes. They were between 8 and 14-years-old. Lt. Halvorsen barely spoke German, but he walked over and tried to talk with them through the fence. One child spoke English, so he told them all the flour, bread, and other cargo the airplanes were bringing the people. During this time, the children were starving, but none of them asked for anything. Usually, Americans in uniform were asked for candy or chocolate, but not one child asked for a single thing. They were simply grateful to finally be freed. Freedom meant everything to them. They knew that food would come, but they were afraid to lose their freedom. He stated, "That's what just blew me away... That was the trigger. I reached into my pocket, but all I had were two sticks of gum. Right then, the smallest decision I made changed the rest of my life.[2]" He reached into his pocket and pulled out two sticks of gum, Wrigley's Doublemint, broke each piece in half and passed the four halves to the children, through the barbed wire. He thought they would all rush for it, but no one did. Those not receiving gum simply asked to smell the wrapper. This so impressed Halvorsen that he made another decision.

He told the children to watch for him and that when he flew over, he would wiggle his wings at them. The children later started calling then Lt. Halverson "Onkel Wackelflugel" or Uncle Wiggly Wings. He also told the children that the next time he landed at Tamplehof he would drop something off to them. Halvorsen returned to the Rhein-Main Air Base, 280 miles away. He and his co-pilot and engineer combined their candy, made handkerchiefs to serve as parachutes and they dropped chocolate and gum to the children. This was the first "Operation Little Vittles" and took place on July 18, 1948. Even though it was illegal to drop food, he continued his service. He flew 100 feet above their heads and dropped the candy bars. In the next three years the drops continued, and the amount of candy donated increased. He was then labeled the "Candy Bomber." (Candy Bomber Delivered Candy, Hope to Berlin, 2018)[3].

Colonel James Haun called Halvorsen in and showed him the newspaper. Halvorsen through he was in a lot of trouble and that the program might be dropped, but to his great relief and joy, the Colonel simply instructed him to continue with the program. Other pilots donated more candy, but they ran out of parachutes. As they looked around, they saw old shirtsleeves, and other fabric so they creatively made parachutes from those. Then, many of the noncommissioned officers and many wives began making them. The Rhein-Main Airforce Base was alive with the thrill of service to bring joy to the hearts of the children. When the American Confectioners Association got involved and donated 18 tons of candy it was a great boon to the program. Students from Chicopee, Massachusetts attached parachutes to them before sending them to Berlin, then to the Westover Air Force Base. 250,000 parachutes and 23 tons of candy were dropped to the children by September 1949. Halvorsen reported that Willie Williams took over for him and dropped even more candy than he had.

"Operation Little Vittles" was a huge success. A little 7-year-old girl named Mercedes wrote a letter saying she loved "Der Schokoladen Flieger," but she noticed her chickens were scared by the planes, thinking they were predator chicken hawks. He never saw her chickens, and 24 years later they met! He was the Templehof commander in the early 1970s. Peter Wild, Mercedes' husband asked the commander to dinner and she showed him the letter that he had written her in 1948. Then, she showed him her chickens. The friendship was later told in Margot Theis Raven's book *Mercedes and the Chocolate Pilot*. (Candy Bomber Delivered Candy, Hope to Berlin, 2018)[4].

In the Salt Lake City, opening ceremonies of the Utah Winter Olympics in 2002 Colonel Halvorsen was part of carrying the German team's national placard in the march. Then, during the 40th and 50th re-enactment celebrations of the anniversaries of "Operation Little Vittles," Colonel Gail Halvorsen was again honored.

On November 22, 2020 Gail Halvorsen was nominated for the Presidential medal of Freedom. https://www.commemorativeairforce.org/news/utah-s-candy-bomber-nominated-for-presidential-medal-of-freedom

The thing I enjoy the most about being the 'Candy Bomber'
is seeing the children's reaction even now
to the idea of a chocolate bar
coming out of the sky," he said. "The most
fun I have is doing air drops
because even here in the states, there's something magical about a
parachute flying out of the sky with a candy bar on it.
Gail Halvorsen

Lesson

When Colonel Halvorsen was known as Lieutenant Halvorsen he was concerned about the children and in awe of their gentleness. When he offered four small pieces of gum, no one grabbed for a piece or complained, instead, the children simply asked that the wrapper could be passed around so they could smell the gum. Even though they were starving and cold their biggest fear was losing their freedom. It is important to realize the sacrifice our troops make every day for our freedoms and safety. As we look throughout history the markers that help us the most are those where genuine acts of service have been offered because someone thought about the situation and how they could make a difference.

The THINK model is simple: Think + Honor + Integrity + Necessity + Kindness

Think: This is possible when you stop, take a deep breath, so you can invite your logical brain to help you analyze and think through the situation or problem.

Honor: To be honorable is to invite trust and altruism which is the concern for the welfare of others. How can you be honorable or benevolent in resolving a conflict or finding a solution? Lt. Halvorsen was honorable and showed great compassion in wanting to find a way to give hope to the children.

Integrity: This is the ability to have a code of ethics and morals and to stay true to those. When you are a man or woman of integrity you are a leader helping others through your example of being responsible and staying true to your word.

Necessity: This is the ability to step back and think, ask yourself "Is this comment really necessary?" Often when we speak from the emotional brain in a negative situation, we hurt others and ourselves. If you stop and think about your comment and ask yourself how important it is, you will save a lot of hurt feelings and have a greater ability to strengthen relationships.

Kindness: This is the culmination of all of these because a person who is kind does not strike out at others in cruelty, they think through things and honor themselves and the other person thereby adhering to their integrity. If a comment is not kind, is it necessary?

Activity

1. What was Lt. Halvorsen most concerned about when he saw the children?

2. Using the THINK model consider a current problem you are having and use it to come to a decision on how to handle it. Write it down by following the model.

   Think – Honor – Integrity – Necessity - Kindness

3. Draw a parachute and inside draw a favorite candy or treat and one message you would like to give children.

4. Share your experience with the class.

   Think – Honor – Integrity – Necessity – Kindness

Footnote

1 "Candy Bomber Delivered Chocolate, Hope to Berlin." (14 September 2018). *Airman Magazine.*

2 Ibid.

3 Ibid.

4 Ibid.

Self-Control Paves the Road to Self-Efficacy

Self-efficacy is the belief in one's ability to influence events that effect one's life and control over the way these events are experienced.
-Albert Bandura

Marshmallows and Self-Control

Occasionally a scientist, psychologist, doctor, or other professional will conduct an outstanding study leading to great insight about human behavior. This was the case when Dr. Walter Mischel conducted what has become widely known as The Marshmallow Experiment. The Bing Nursery School at Stanford University provided the setting for the study. It was in the 1960s. Dr. Mischel's team had a bag of marshmallows and each child was given one with the instructions that they eat it immediately or wait. They would be left alone in a room for a few minutes and if the child had not eaten it they could have two treats when the researcher returned. A bell was available for the child to ring if they wanted to eat the marshmallow before the researcher came back, and if they rang the bell, they would not receive the second treat, Konikova (2014)[1].

The results of this simple experiment taught Dr. Mischel a lot about self-control. He found that if a child could delay gratification, and the longer they could wait, then the better they would do later in life in measures he called executive function. The children who delayed eating the marshmallow had higher grades, performed better in other areas of school, earned more money, were wealthier as adults and happier! They were also less likely to engage in negative self-defeating behaviors such as crime, drug abuse, alcoholism, and obesity, Konikova (2014)[2].

The study continued for fifty years. He discovered that there was one consistent factor in those children delaying gratification. It was their ability to alter their perception of the object, for the first study it was the marshmallow. It generalized over to other behaviors. That ability to stop and wait, to delay getting what one wants, is a powerful indicator for personal success. For instance, one boy simply could not wait, but they taught him how to by visualizing the marshmallow as a picture, not a real marshmallow. This helped him to learn to abstain from immediate gratification and impetuous behaviors. Dr. Mischel asked him how he learned to stop and wait until it was time to each the marshmallow. He replied, "You can't eat a picture." (Konikova, 2014)[3]. Others would avoid eating the food by putting it away or keeping it at a distance, and one other recommendation was to picture it as something else, a marshmallow could be a cloud.

Lesson

Learning self-control generalizes to all areas of your life. If you learn self-control you will be healthier, you will exercise and eat more nutritious food. You will have more friends because others will not be leery of your anger or manipulations. You will learn more because your ability to focus will increase. You will be stronger within because you have exerted patience and you have shown that you are able and willing to wait to get things. This is called delayed gratification. Learning this skill also makes a person emotionally stronger and more resilient. Instead of viewing a situation as an insurmountable crisis, they learn to stop, think about different responses and options, and make better decisions. By learning this skill, you will be emotionally stronger. This is part of that which is called character, which includes our beliefs, perceptions, and patterns in the way we treat others. It also includes our integrity, and values.

Activity

1. Fill in the chart.
2. Discuss as a class.

Jan Booth, M.S.

Mastering Self-Control

WANTS	NEEDS	CHARACTER BENEFITS

Footnote

1   Konikova, M. (9 October, 2014). The Struggles of a Psychologist Studying Self-Control. *New Yorker.*

2   Ibid.

3   Ibid.

Lesson 11

Following MY Inner Compass

How far you go in life depends on your being tender with the young, compassionate with the aged, sympathetic with the striving and tolerant of the weak and strong. Because someday in your life you will have been all of these.
-George Washington Carver

From Slavery to Freedom and Brilliance

The infant was born into slavery, with the exact date not known, but was estimated to be in 1864, in Diamond, Missouri. Moses Carver was his "master," the man who bought and owned him. Tragically, when he was just one week old "night raiders" kidnapped George, his mother, and his sister. George was located and raised by Moses and Susan Carver, who loved him and raised their own child. They encouraged him in his education and love for learning.

When he was about twelve, he was given the opportunity to attend a school for black people (African Americans) 10 miles south of his town. He was thrilled! When he arrived, the school was closed for the night, so he slept in a barn. It is interesting to note that many times good people showed up in George's life, helping him succeed in accomplishing his goals and encouraging him to invite new dreams. For instance, the next day George met Mariah Watkins, a kind woman who rented him a room. He went by the name of "Carver's George" and she told him now to go by the name George Carver. This gave him independence and dispelled the slave mentality. Ms. Watkins told George, "You must learn all you can, then go back out into the world and give your learning back to the people." George Washington Carver Facts for Kids (2019)[1] provided the details for this lesson.

George was motivated to learn all he could and to make a difference. At the age of 13, he relocated to another foster family's home in Fort Scott, Kansas and continued attending a variety of schools until he graduated from the Minneapolis High School in Minneapolis, Kansas.

Even though slavery was abolished, sadly, people still held a lot of prejudice. George applied to many colleges before he was finally accepted into the Highland University located in Highland, Kansas. But, when he arrived, he was again rejected, simply because of his race. Still, undeterred by his many setbacks, and instead of retaliating or spending his life with hatred he just kept pursuing his dream of getting more education and making a difference. So, in August of 1886 George traveled Eden Township, Kansas where he established a claim on a homestead. He kept a small conservatory, or nursery of plant, and later transferred them to a 17-acre farm which he maintained by himself.

George proved himself to be responsible, hard-working, and a great seeker of knowledge. In 1888 he was able to obtain a $300.00 bank loan for education and by June he left the area. In 1890 he studied art and piano at the Simpson College in Indianola, Iowa. Later, he continued his research at the Iowa Experiment Station under the direction of Louis Pammel and Joseph Budd. He completed a Master's Degree and gained national recognition for his work on plant pathology and mycology and received his master's degree of science in 1896 where he also became the first African American faculty member for Iowa State University.

George was a man of honor and great intellect. Booker T. Washington invited him to head the Agriculture Department at the Tuskegee Institute in 1896, where he taught for the next 47 years. He made the department a research center, teaching crop rotation methods, he introduced different alternative cash crops to improve soils, and initiated research into the production of crop products and encouraged and taught self-sufficiency. Carver was a scientist, but he was also a kind and concerned man. By exemplifying integrity, hard work, and commitment to excellence, George Washington Carver empowered his students towards the fruition of their goals. He even compiled a list of eight specific virtues or characteristics his students were instructed to incorporate into their own characters and personalities.

(The following list taken directly from https://kids.kiddle.co/George Washington Carver)

- Be clean both inside and out.
- Neither look up to the rich nor down on the poor.
- Lose, if need be, without squealing.
- Win without bragging.
- Always be considerate of women, children, and older people.
- Be too brave to lie.
- Be too generous to cheat.
- Take your share of the world and let others take theirs.

Another creative idea of George's was to have a mobile classroom to take education to the farmers, which he called the "Jesup wagon" named after the New York philanthropist and financier Morris Ketchum Jesup who had provided the funding for the program.

In a U. S. World War II poster of 1943, he was pictured and listed as "One of America's Great Scientists." At this time he was known as George Washington Carver. On January 5, 1943 George Washington Carver died from complications he incurred from falling down his stairs. He was 78 years old. George was buried next to his mentor and friend, Booker T. Washington at Tuskegee University. His tombstone stated: *He could have added fortune to fame, but caring for neither, he found happiness and honor in being helpful to the world.*[3] A few of his several honors are listed below. (George Washington Carver Facts for Kids).

Lesson

Each of us has that inner drive towards something we are interested in. Unfortunately, we may feel discouraged and that drive gets diminished. At that point we have the choice. Are we going to dismiss our goals through negative, self-defeating thinking and actions, or dig deeper to find the courage and strength within to stay on course? George Washington Carver is an excellent example of someone who had a thirst for knowledge and a passion for agriculture, which eventually took him into the annals of history. He never gave up.

Assignment

1. George Washington Carver overcame many challenges. Discuss three of them.
2. What challenges have held you back from achieving your goals?
3. Write an essay on something you need to overcome and how you are going to do that in a manner that results in your future success and in helping others?

Footnotes

1   George Washington Carver Facts for Kids. *Kiddle Encyclopedia.* Found online (16 December 2019) from https://kids.kiddle.co/George_Washington_Carver.

2   Ibid.

3   Ibid.

Lesson 12

Understanding What is Important and Real

*When the soul is fed the spirit is strengthened,
when the spirit is strengthened the body knows peace,
and when the body knows peace the individual's capacity
to give and receive love is enhanced exponentially
bringing light to soften the trials of mortality for others.*
-Jan C. Booth

Getting to the Heart of Self by Knowing What is Real

"What is REAL?" asked the Rabbit one day, when they were lying side by side near the nursery fender, before Nana came to tidy the room. "Does it mean having things that buzz inside you and a stick-out handle?"

"Real isn't how you are made," said the Skin Horse. "It's a thing that happens to you. When a child loves you for a long, long time, not just to play with, but REALLY loves you, then you become Real."

"Does it hurt?" asked the Rabbit.

"Sometimes," said the Skin Horse, for he was always truthful. "When you are Real you don't mind being hurt."

"Does it happen all at once, like being wound up," he asked, "or bit by bit?"

"It doesn't happen all at once," said the Skin Horse. "You become. It takes a long time. That's why it doesn't happen often to people who break easily, or have sharp edges, or who have to be carefully kept. Generally, by the time you are Real, most of your hair has been loved off, and your eyes drop out and you get loose in the joints and very shabby. But these things don't matter at all, because once you are Real you can't be ugly, except to people who don't understand."

"I suppose *you* are real?" said the Rabbit. And then he wished he had not said it, for he thought the Skin Horse might be sensitive. But the Skin Horse only smiled.

"The Boy's Uncle made me Real," he said. "That was a great many years ago; but once you are Real you can't become unreal again. It lasts for always."

The Rabbit sighed. He thought it would be a long time before this magic called Real happened to him. He longed to become Real, to know what it felt like; and yet the idea of growing shabby and losing his eyes and whiskers was rather sad. He wished that he could become it without these uncomfortable things happening to him. (Williams, 1991, pgs. 5-6)[1].

Lesson

To be authentic and real requires humility and the willingness to be teachable. It is allowing the true self to be involved in the relationship or situations. The bunny longed to become real, but the horse had, and he knew the beauty of being loved and the wear and tear involved in relationships. The risk is worth the pain and the benefits of having honest and real relationships are those which gird us up when times get hard. Notice what the horse said why people don't allow that depth of giving and sharing, loving and trust, "…That's why it doesn't happen often to people who break easily, or have sharp edges, or who have to be carefully kept." If one has been hurt and refuses to bond or attach to others in the future it will only hurt themselves. If one is caustic and angry their ability to maintain healthy relationships is damaged, and if one gets hurt over every incident or is inclined towards drama and catastrophic thinking it invites unhealthy relationships and attachment.

Due to personal circumstances and one's own personality different areas of healthy relationships may be challenging and one's ability to be empowered and be part of one is hampered. Interpersonal relationships take work, honesty, loyalty, healthy boundaries, kindness and patience. All of those factors invite in the "REAL" part. Ways that people forfeit kind and lasting relationships are through addiction, another depression or anxiety, and someone else anger, self-destructive behaviors, sarcasm, and cruelty. The problem is not having the challenge but is in not taking the steps to overcome the issue. Consider the military lieutenant going through intense training to do his job and in doing so, he or she needs to follow every rule, go by the book so to speak. Now, let's add in the personality characteristics of impatience and quick to anger. The combination of factors can be tough because they have learned order, obedience, and following regulations. When things are not quite as they feel they should be their gut reaction might be anger, and if uncontrolled, may quickly turn to rage.

An example of this is John, a young man with a history of violence. He was put on probation and could only continue in his career if he attended anger management classes. There, he learned the importance of mindfulness, the very act of stopping, taking several slow breaths and calming himself. He visualized a place of peace and did this daily for eight weeks! His wife attended the classes with him so she could learn the skills and help him to be successful in actually changing. This strengthened their marriage.

The end of the eight-week course was coming. John was observed in different settings at work. One day he was making a delivery for his company and the supply supervisor named Mark, at the local hospital was taking a long time before helping him. He reverted back to his old habits and started to get mad. The man was on the phone and knew he was there, "How dare he take my time! How dare he ignore me and keep talking when he can see me right in front of him" he murmured to himself. Then, he remembered how anger had almost gotten him fired. He remembered how close he had come to losing his wife because of his anger, and he remembered his visualized place of peace.

This was the turning point for him. He paused and waited while he visualized himself being calm and could feel the anger leave him. He wisely started to plan out his day to give him something else to focus on. Then, there was silence. He looked up at the man, the same man he had been furious with only moments before had tears streaming down his face. He quietly put the phone down, then looked at John and apologized for making him wait. "Mark, are you ok? What's wrong," asked John with genuine concern. "My wife and I have been waiting for her to be able to have a liver transplant and she just got word there was one ready for her. She'll go to surgery tonight."

John was filled with compassion. He asked Mark more questions, could he leave work now? How could he help? Mark told him he was off work in a half hour and would rush to catch the bus to get across town, hopefully in time to be with his wife before surgery. John called his boss and asked permission to help this man. He told him the whole story and was told to take care of Mark first and complete the deliveries later in the day or the next day. John and the Mark became lifetime friends. He and his wife helped both of them through the weeks of waiting for the wife to recover. They organized dinners for them and helped with their children.

John learned first-hand the meaning of compassion, the gift of patience, and the joy of service and becoming "real."

What a powerful lesson it is to walk in another's shoes for a moment, but the key is to calm down enough to do so. When we see things through another's eyes it makes such a difference. For John, he had to learn new ways to respond instead of reacting to things. The hidden factor in this was that John's anger stemmed from a history of trauma and child abuse. He wanted to succeed but his unresolved grief had molded into rage and the rage destroyed all previous relationships he had been in. This was his fourth job in two years, but it was his favorite because he felt that the company truly cared about him. In learning self-control and emotion regulation John was able to be the light on the hill for Mark and his wife. He stayed with the company and within five years had been promoted to management. Instead of living a life of failed relationships and job changes he was enjoying a life of personal success because he had been humbled enough to understand what was real and how to honor his authentic self.

Activity

1. Take a series of five slow breaths in, then exhale for the count of seven.
2. Picture a place of peace and serenity.
3. Draw this out as you picture your safe and peaceful setting.
4. Discuss how the breathing and visualization felt.

Footnotes

1   Williams, M. (nd) *The velveteen rabbit*. [E-reader version]. NY: Open Road Integrated Media. Retrieved from smile.amazon.com.

Lesson 13

Emotional Stability – Control Over Emotional Rollercoasters

Our thinking creates a pathway to success or failure.
By disclaiming responsibility for our present,
we crush the prospect of an incredible
future that might have been ours.
Andy Andrews – The Traveler's Gift[1]

Maria, An Anchor of Faith

Maria was wheeled into the Newborn Intensive Care Unit. Her husband was her anchor, and both were filled with worry over their critically ill newborn. Over the next few weeks, the newborn received different interventions. The mother was amazing. Despite just having a baby, she recovered quickly and was emotionally strong, but what was most striking was her spirituality. She glowed with faith, hope, and love. The medical staff noticed a difference in the NBICU when she was visiting her baby. There was a profound increased influence of peace and joy that filled the room. She adored her little son, bringing in toys and books to read and share with him along with cuddly stuffed animals to comfort him when she was away.

Maria was a woman of faith. She walked in faith. She walked in peace. She walked in a greater awareness of the power of a higher being helping her. She never discussed the origin of her spiritual depth, but it radiated within her and embraced anyone nearby. She was a foundation of comfort to those working to keep her baby alive. She was a source of peace to the little boy struggling to live, and she was a symbol of strength to her family.

Sadly, the baby died before he reached the age of one. He never got to go home, but the mother brought home to the infant. The setting did not matter, for the mother created that place of peace her little boy would fold into every time she visited. She was a woman of control. She had control over her emotions for she had nurtured seeds of faith and peace in her daily life. She understood that she may only have this infant a short time and she grabbed every second to extend love and comfort to him. When the baby's father visited, he exuded the same comfort and peace to all. Of course, they grieved for the struggles they saw their baby endure and for the loss of him when he passed, but in their grief, they still found the strength to bring a sense of calm to all who surrounded them, and to comfort their little one regardless of the circumstances.

They did not let the roller coaster of emotion throw them off the track of their lives. Instead, they took the time with their infant to bask in their love for him and present a respite of love, hope, and warmth. Their examples of spiritual depth, of soulfulness, was a gift to all who worked with them. When he died, their legacy of faith lived on, strengthening family, friends, and hospital personnel.

Lesson

Emotional awareness is key to emotional control. Awareness of thoughts, feelings, and concerns of those around you. And, as you know, emotions are like roller coasters with many twists and turns, ups and downs. The key is to learn to self-anchor so that you don't fly off the seat and create chaos, or land in the muck, which may take years to come out of. Anne Curran's (2010) work on trauma lends insight into its effects and the often over-whelming feelings of sadness that follow. "Some common reactions during sadness are heavy eyelids: rising cheeks; tightening sensation or a lump in the throat; watery eyes. People differ in how they experience sadness, knowing your own process and how it may differ from those you care about may help you better understand some of the miscommunications and misinterpretations that may occur or may have occurred in your life. (Curran, 2010, p. 101)[2]

What emotions play out in your day-to-day life? How much control you do you have over them? What do you even know about emotions? Emotions are a major part of problem-solving and decision making. Emotions can make the boy a man, the girl a woman, or they can control the person thereby inhibiting their own personal empowerment and progress. Emotions can strengthen character or take the person hostage. Learning what emotions are, and how to recognize them is a primary factor in strengthening resiliency and learning how to take personal control over one's emotional striations. Emotions are not just isolated to the individual but are seen played out in everyday life. Some characteristics of being emotionally aware and self-controlled adults include the ability to be adaptable to their surroundings, they are assertive, not aggressive. They calm themselves, control their thoughts, and actions. The key is to be self-aware and learn how to live in a manner which invites success, reinforces patience, and strengthens one's commitment to excellence.

Activity

1. Consider the list below and check those which apply to you and circle those characteristics you are willing to learn to incorporate into your life.
2. Draw a picture of a roller coaster.
3. Draw and color the surrounding scene, are there clouds? Flowers? Animals? People? Use colors to further emphasize your emotional rollercoaster.
4. Now, list different emotions and choose colors for each emotion you experience and put them throughout the roller coaster.

Jan Booth, M.S.

5. Discuss the feelings of "out of control" emotions. Highlight the emotions you feel you have in the list below.
6. Breathing Routine. Inhale for the count of 3, hold for 4, exhale slowly to the count of 3, repeat this 3 times.

Characteristics of Emotionally Aware Adults

Flexible	Assertive, not Aggressive
Ability to Self-Soothe	Emotional Awareness
Kind and Generous	Caring and Compassionate
Self-Disciplined	Empathetic
Self & Other Forgiveness	Peace Seeker
Integrity-Based/Honors Self & Others	Maintain Healthy Boundaries
Recognizes Toxic Relationships	Accountable & Responsible
Excellent Listening Skills	Loved and Loving
Internally Motivated	Thinks Optimistically
Seeks Peace	Finds Solutions

Footnotes

1 Andy Andrews (2002). *The Traveler's Gift.* Nashville, TE. W. Publishing Group, p. 26
2 Curran, L. A. (2010) *Trauma Competency. A Clinician's Guide.* PESI: Eau Claire, WI.

Lesson 14

Patience: The Key to Anger Management

Anger is never without a reason,
but seldom with a good one.
Benjamin Franklin

Nails in the Fence

The father loved his son and recognized a challenge in his little boy so one day he instructed him to take a bag of nails and a hammer, then, every time he lost his temper, he was told to hammer one nail into the fence. This little boy had a difficult time managing his anger. His parents had tried to teach him patience through discipline and talking, but nothing worked so his father decided on a clever object lesson; having him hammer nails into a fence, The Fence (2010)[1].

On the first day 37 nails had been slammed into that fence! 37 explosive outbursts from that little boy! Gradually, over the next few weeks, the boy recognized how destructive his anger was and slowly learned to control it. Each day less nails were added to the disarray of spilled out anger. Slowly he discovered that it was actually easier to remain calm and keep control over his temper than it was to hammer nails into a fence. One day, the little boy didn't hammer one single nail! He was experiencing self-confidence and a realization of self-efficacy, a belief in himself and his ability to take control over his emotions. He had not lost his temper once. He rushed to his father with excitement, but his father surprised him. "Son, now I want you to go and pull out one nail for each day you control your temper." Days and weeks passed until all the nails were finally removed.

The big lesson came when the father gently took his little boy's hand and led him to the fence to see all the holes. "The fence will never be the same again," his father wisely told him. Then he taught him the power of words, that saying mean things always left a scar, and losing one's temper never helped others, instead, it hurt them. He told him that even if he said he was sorry the wound was still there until the person was able to heal on their own. Harsh words just leave scars, The Fence (2010)[2].

The little boy learned a lesson that lasted him a lifetime, a lesson provided by a loving, wise father who chose to discipline with wisdom and love rather than anger and punishment.

Lesson

Effective communication requires self-control, patience, creativity, humility, commitment, and the willingness to learn how to communicate. Difficult conversations invite each of these principles. The boy learned a hard lesson. Each nail he hammered into the fence represented his moments of anger and when he removed them, he could see the damage to the board. Often, we do not stop to think of the long-term consequences of uncontrolled anger, sarcasm, or other thoughtless comments and we may not readily see the wounds we have left. This lesson invites you to consider whether you want to be a person of kindness and integrity, someone others can trust and depend upon to show compassion and tenderness, or do you want to keep others away, which keeps you in a box of isolation. When that is happening the person, in essence, has a wall around themselves. That wall of protection they often use through anger, sarcasm, and other words of cruelty is a means for them to feel like they have the upper hand, that they are powerful, but in the end, they are left feeling vulnerable and rejected, perhaps even unlovable.

There are many dimensions to becoming an effective communicator, but the bottom line is, are you willing to listen, really listen with your ears, heart, mind, and soul? Are you humble and patient enough to keep your reactionary comments in check and simply allow yourself to breathe slowly and efficiently, calmly, and to gather information, and then have a healthy conversation? This can be verbally, in texts, emails, and on social media. Which image do you want to project? Hate breeds hatred, anger breeds hostility, but love invites true communication that can improve relationships and create a healthier environment for all. Loving relationships strengthen the core soulfulness of each person involved, which brings light and hope, and offers the bridge of connection to guide others through turbulent seasons of life.

Activity

1. Think of a situation that angered you and I encourage you to practice this each day. Imagine it as a circle of emotion and you are in the center of it. Now, visualize yourself stepping out of it. Leave the anger in the circle.
2. Label the emotions you felt in addition to anger.
3. Design a wall. Label the materials you would use and include colors.
4. Put yourself behind the wall.
5. On the wall list the ways you push people away through various styles of communication. Examples would be anger, hostility, frustration, irritability, depression, negative thinking, anger outbursts, sarcasm, etc.
6. As a class discuss reasons for anger. There are always other emotions involved. List these.
7. Discuss a time you felt great remorse for your anger.
   Now go back to step one. Again, walk out of the circle of emotion Breathe deeply 3 times (In for the count of 3, hold for 4, release for 3, hold for 4, repeat)

8. Visualize putting the anger in a balloon and letting it float away.
9. Breathe in peace. This allows the logical brain to become more dominant than the emotional brain and can help you break the cycle of anger.

Footnotes

1   The Fence. (7 November, 2010). TEACHNET.COM Retrieved from http://teachnet.com/communicate/inspiration/story-the-fence/
2   Ibid.

Lesson 15

It Is Up to Me - Overcoming the Odds

There are moments when troubles enter our lives
and we can do nothing to avoid them.
But they are there for a reason.
Only when we have overcome them will we
Understand why they were there.
Paul Coelho

Burned

The flame exploded before his eyes, he raced out of the garage screaming in pain and fear. John had accidentally caught his garage on fire, and the fire quickly enveloped his body in flames. His brother rushed to his side, grabbed a floor mat, and laid it over him to put out the flames, saving his life. His sister ran in the house and got cold water to pour over him, his other sister held him. John wrote about that moment when he was shivering in shock, lying in the snow and hearing his brother, Jim, cry out, "…John, wake up! Stay awake! You can't go to sleep!" (O'Leary, p. 75)[1] Jim could have jumped back from the flames as they burned his hands, but he didn't. He stayed with John. His sister comforted him, "It's going to be ok John. It's going to be ok. Have faith and fight, (O'Leary, p. 75)[2].

His young siblings were there to help him through the initial stages of the crisis, and they stayed by his side emotionally throughout his recovery. How much damage was caused? His legs were severely burned, and his fingers essentially burned off. The flame did not reach his face. For that he was very grateful.

This is the story of a child who endured intense emotional and physical trauma and subsequent pain. John O'Leary was faced with choices on each step of his journey and in those defining moments, which he labeled as ***inflection points***, John took his experiences and used them to teach others of courage, tenacity, and the will to live. "Because of the fire, I don't take things for granted, am grateful for each day, and am certain that the best is yet to come." (O'Leary, P. XI)[3]

John's mother played a critical role in his recovery. When she arrived at the emergency room she rushed into her son and asked him, "Do you want to die? It's your choice," (O'Leary, 2016, p. 5)[4]. John immediately realized that his future was up to him. His mother could not remove the pain or turn back time to save her son from the fire, but she could be honest with him and let him know that he had power.

John believed that personal accountability was essential for character development and success in life. It forces the person to "own" his or her life, to be the captain and not just float along at the whim of others. John's mother was a huge factor in this, too. Can you imagine how relieved and excited he was to leave the hospital and go home to his family? Little did he know another surprise was in store for him.

The call for dinner arrived and John was glad to have a home cooked meal. He sat in his chair, looked at the food and his utensils and asked himself how on earth he was going to eat with his hands bandaged and fingers missing? Immediately, his sister, Amy, reached over to help him but again his mother stepped in with her blunt verbiage telling him that if he wanted to eat, he would just have to figure it out! Wow! That may seem harsh, but as you dig deeper you recognize the profound message his wise mother was giving him: if you want to be in charge of your own life you have to be the one to take care of you. In no way was his mother cruel or thoughtless; quite the opposite, she was so filled with love and wisdom for her son that she had to put her feelings on hold and push him to be the man she knew that little boy could one day become. Later, John stated, "Our individual strengths and weaknesses are typically just different sides of the same coin." (O'Leary, 2016, p. 40)[5].

John believed in living a radically and profoundly inspiring life, to be a person who brings humor, joy, and hope to others by encouraging people to embrace their story and celebrate the miracle of being themselves. He drew on his inner strengths and faith. He learned that he had courage he had never before recognized. He learned that even though others pushed him hard it was because they cared about him. And he learned that many tender gifts of service came his way when he most needed them, those critical moments when someone walked into his room at just the right time to keep him going. Jack Buck told him, "Kid, wake up!" (O'Leary, 2016, p. 248)[6]. Some made him do physical therapy, others offered incentives, and all showed concern. His parents and siblings showered him with loving attention, but his mother was tough, in a loving and wise way.

John's father gave him unconditional love and support, then in his final years, John looked to his father's strength to help him continue his journey as a man. His father battled Parkinson's disease and John learned even more about the journey of facing challenges by observing the struggles his father endured through the afflictions of his disease.

Another person of influence was his doctor, Dr. Ayvazian, who told him that even if he could not do everything others did, he could still do magnificent things. Even if he couldn't play baseball, which John loved, he could own a team and be part of the game. He taught him great lessons in looking at possibilities rather than focusing on the deterrents and obstacles. His physical therapist and forced him to walk. The pain was horrifying but he never gave up on John and somehow John never gave up on himself. His nurse, Roy, was relentless in helping him, stating, "Boy, you are going to walk again. I'll walk with you," O'Leary (2016, p. 138)[7].

One day the door to his hospital room opened and in walked Glenn Cunningham, a silver Olympic medalist who had also suffered severe burns as a child. He was another person who taught John to believe in himself. Glenn shared that his burns were so severe that his mother would carry him to the fence surrounding his yard and leave him to stand on his own. When he fell, she would carry him back in the house. Slowly, but steadily, the strength in his legs increased and he was able to stand on his own and eventually walk. Mr. Cunningham's own experience with severe burns gave John strength and fortitude.

John had to learn how to write, a difficult task without fingers. How did John learn to write in spite of having no fingers? He received baseballs signed by famous players. If he wanted another one, he would have to write a thank you note, which he did, and accumulated a lot of valuable baseballs, but the greatest value was in the incentive each signed ball offered a little boy to rise above his handicap. John said, "We may not control everything that happens to us, but we always control how we respond," O'Leary (2016, p. 12)[8].

In another instance an elderly woman talked to him firmly, "John, listen to me. You need to wake up. Your family needs you to lead them. It's time to wake up now. No more living idly. No more excuses. No more sleep walking. It's time to wake up[7]!" (O'Leary, 2016, p. 247)[9].

Now, as an adult John offers help in a variety of ways. He travels to different communities to give motivational speeches. One day he visited a prison and told the inmates, "I want you men to think of three things that you are thankful for. More specifically, three things you are grateful for because of your time in prison," (O'Leary, 2016, pgs. 119-123)[10]. One inmate stood up and had a list of thirty-one things that immediately came to his mind! No matter our circumstances, when we focus on gratitude our hearts and minds will be full.

Stretching leads to growth.
Growth is frequently painful.
But "growth is the only evidence of life."
-John O'Leary

Lesson

No matter where we are on our journey, we have the choice to move forward or stay locked into our present circumstances, but remember life is not stagnant. If you stay locked into only one way of thinking, you will regress. Think of a time you or someone you know broke their leg or arm. The muscles atrophied and they had trouble moving. They had to do a lot of work to get those muscles working properly. This is how it is with our spirits and drive. If we are not moving forward, we are sliding backwards. An example is dealing with severe depression, addiction, or other mental health challenges. It is very hard to even make the choice to get well when the mind and body are depleted, but the truth is, one little decision to do one thing differently each day can lead to a myriad of choices that will empower that person towards health and productivity.

Activity

1. Write an essay on a critical time in your life where you were given the opporutnity to make the choice to move forward with principles of success and achievement or to continue in a life filled with pain and regrets.
2. Draw that out. You can use symbols or yourself, caught in that web of pain and sorrow, anger, and hostility.
3. Now, draw a bridge, which represents a way to escape the past and cross the bridge.
4. Add in the most peaceful scene you can imagine.
5. List the qualities it took to move out of the past and into the future.
6. Share with others.

Footnotes

1   O'Leary, J. (2016). *On fire: The 7 choices to ignite a radically inspired life.* NY: Gallery Books.
2   Ibid.

Jan Booth, M.S.

3   Ibid.
4   Ibid.
5   Ibid.
6   Ibid.
7   Ibid.
8   Ibid.
9   Ibid.
10   Ibid.

Lesson 16

Rising Above Emotional Toxicity– How Personal Struggles Can Empower You to Greatness

Obstacles don't have to stop you. If you run into a wall, don't turn around and give up. Figure out how to climb it, go through it, or work around it.
-Michael Jordan

Staci – A Woman of Strength and Emotional Resiliency

The woman came in as a student of learning. She was intelligent, articulate, and knowledgeable. As I heard her story, I was amazed at the resiliency with which I saw her rise above her past and embrace her future. Instead of focusing her attention on graduation and beyond she was enjoying the journey, and empowering others through her insights. This is her story.

Staci was adopted into a family where her parents did not have a solid attachment relationship with her. She had everything she needed physically, the family was financially successful, but she was missing those important ingredients of unconditional love and belonging. She grew up feeling she was not of worth. Her trust of others was damaged and her ability to quickly adapt to new situations hindered. As an adult she was articulate, intelligent, well-read, committed to excellence, and most importantly, a woman with heart. She cared. She worked to become a therapist to help others so that they could overcome the heartaches they had suffered through life. She was and is an exceptional woman.

Let's review more of her story because it takes great insight and determination to get well and Staci certainly had mastered both. In her autobiography she wrote that she was a workaholic teen, this kept her from facing her grief and trauma because there was no one who would get her the help she needed. She left home two weeks after she turned 18, and that is when rebellion set in. She was falling apart internally, a type of implosion beginning, the memories were creeping up and they were terrifying, so she turned to alcohol, which numbed her pain. Her mental health was declining, she married when she was 21. Her husband was in the military and returned from Iraq with severe PTSD. Because of his own issues coupled with hers, their marriage did not work out.

Staci suffered with depression and anxiety but was able to get herself sober despite the internal demons. Eventually she remarried and had a child but her second husband was an addict. True to her strength, she stayed sober, but still lived with the issues that led her to drink the first time. She had unfinished grief and confusion inside of her. Staci could find no release for her pain and fears yet garnered the energy and strength to focus on raising her child with love and security. She was the one to work and carry the responsibilities of the family. Then, life caught up with her. Four different times she had to be hospitalized when she could no longer cope with the demands of daily living. Initially, she was hospitalized for weeks, stabilized, and returned home to raise her daughter, but the cycles repeated. Each hospitalization provided her with additional education and insight into herself and others and took less time to get calmed. Eventually she moved beyond her pain and into the field of leading others to wellness. Staci's courage and tenacity provide a testament not only to her strength, but to the divine light of hope and power for goodness within each of us if we but nurture it. She wrote the following insights for this lesson.

"From the 1st hospitalization, I started my journey into understanding my mental health and illness. Even though I still had 3 more major events each time was more enlightening, and also through outpatient therapy I really began to see that my life meant more than the way I was living. I knew how crappy I felt with my life and keeping my daughter in that situation would only show her that that was what to expect from life. The last time I was in a hospital and after some interactions with another patient, the head psychiatrist told me she thought I should pursue a career in the mental health field, I had a gift for seeing things in others and myself in a way that she thought would be so beneficial to myself and the community. I left that last time with a renewed sense of self-confidence because of a lot of what the therapist had told me. I knew I had changed my mindset and now it was time to change my life and that meant big life changes."[1]

Staci returned to school, got divorced and started to show her daughter that there was joy and great purpose in life. She slowly learned to let go of the past, as she said, "…sometimes it's ok to let go of things that are just so very toxic." Staci's love for her daughter pushed her to establish goals and work towards them while offering her daughter a life of hope and joy. She is a wonderful mother, one who is devoted to her daughter and part of that is keeping herself sober, safe, and mentally healthy.

Education provided her an outlet, a focus, experience, knowledge, and forward momentum. She is now able to evaluate her life and situations as they arrive. She has support people she can turn to, and mental health interventions as needed. She has developed and nurtured confidence in herself. She has found that she is a woman of great worth and a mother with infinite love and devotion to her child. She has a keen sense of humor, which brings joy to her daughter, friends, and associates.

Staci continues to have a unique ability to handle major stresses well. However, sometimes the day-to-day irritants are hard on her. At times depression and anxiety seem to envelope her and even getting out of bed can be a challenge. She is still dealing with the traumas of childhood and the fifteen-year marriage to a "rageaholic" drug addict which forced her to be hyper-vigilant. These have taken a toll on her, but she continues moving forward. She has a great capacity for compassion and the motivation to help others, and her future goal of being a therapist, once realized, will offer her clients a person of empathy, intellect, sensitivity, wisdom, and commitment.

Lesson

Studying the challenges and struggles others have endured is one way of finding the strength within to carry on. Life requires balance and balance calls upon the innermost parts of self to find those places of peace, harmony, positive intention, and soulfulness.

Staci is a woman with courage, determination, and spunk. Her ability to see what needs to change is remarkable, and the courage she has called upon to do so is exemplary. Though she lived through a lot of trauma, she not only survived it, but has moved into greatness as a woman, mother, and friend.

The ability to rise above one's challenges is the common denominator for each of us. Some will choose to do so and live a life of kindness, compassion, and altruism, as with Staci. Others will look for the easy way out through addictions, criminal behavior or just giving up and having others take care of them. To deeper your own understanding and gain another perspective of your own life I invite you to complete the following activities.

Activities

1. Draw a picture of yourself. (It can be a stick figure).
2. Around each picture write your strengths and challenges.

3. Use specific colors to represent the different points written.
4. Draw a picture of someone you admire.
5. List their strengths and challenges.
6. As a class discuss how others have overcome their challenges.

Footnote

1   Private interview and correspondence, with permission to share, anonymity maintained.

Lesson 17

The Healing Power of Forgiveness -

To forgive is to set a prisoner free
and discover that the prisoner was you.
-Lewis B. Smedes

Forgiveness Was Her Miracle

Corrie Ten Boom was a valiant and courageous woman. She joined with her father and family to fight the Nazis in World War II by hiding Jewish refugees in their home. After a period of time they were discovered and Corrie, her sister, and father were sent to concentration camps. Her father and sister eventually died, but Corrie's faith in God was stronger than any force. There was one guard who was a major catalyst in the death of her sister, and she had a difficult time forgiving him. I know this happens no matter who you are. There are always people who will help you and others who are caustic and thrive on being mean and difficult. Corrie had a real dilemma because she had traveled across the globe preaching forgiveness, yet she knew she harbored ill feelings towards that one particular guard who had caused the death of her sister. After all, her family had been killed by the Nazis, her life had been shattered, and she carried a lot of trauma deep inside herself. But Corrie had faith and had spent many years teaching and ministering to people about forgiveness and love. She taught others with great warmth and joy and wrote books and sermons that brought light and hope into the lives of others.

Corrie had not returned to Germany for twenty years and realized that it was time to do so. One day she was preaching in a beautiful German chapel and noticed a man standing at the back of the room. She immediately recognized him as the Nazi guard who had brought death and pain to so many others, including her sister. She flashed back to him in his uniform and hatred seemed to enter her soul. Her sermon was finished. Everyone left but the guard! He was actually waiting for her! Can you imagine the fear in her heart? The anguish and terrible thoughts of animosity consuming her? As she was greeting everyone and wishing them well, she knew she would soon come face to face with this man who symbolized all the pain she had suffered. Finally, there he was. Waiting. Next in line. What a burden it was! How could she get out of this situation? She could not run away, nor did she choose to yell at him, though she probably wanted him arrested right there on the spot! Instead, she turned to the Lord, to the Spirit or Higher Power she clung to, and prayed. She did not kneel down and pray, she humbly stood and prayed for help. Suddenly she felt a tiny electric shock, a positive power beyond her own, lift her arm. She extended her shaking hand of forgiveness to him and she felt the waves of hatred leave and the gift of pure peace enter her heart. At last, she was freed. Through her belief system, which for her was the Lord, she was able to truly forgive him and from that she was forever healed from the wounds inflicted upon her so long ago, Ten Boom (2006)[1].

Lesson

Forgiveness is demanding, difficult, and sometimes seemingly impossible to achieve, but this lesson offers a new approach to forgiveness. I ask you to view it as a process. Yes, forgiveness is a process, and you can begin it today. You do not have to expect yourself to be completely freed from anger or to think that by forgiving someone you are saying what they did to you was all right. In no way is that part of forgiveness. It is a process of releasing the toxins it holds in your body. Forgiveness is for you, for your spiritual, emotional, and physical health. It is your way of inviting inner peace and soothing tranquility. It is a journey of letting go and it is your gift to give yourself.

Activities

1. Draw a symbol to represent forgiveness, anger, resentment, and vulnerability. This can be a heart, circle, square, star, or anything else you can visualize.
2. Using colors to represent your feeling(s), pour all your energy into filling in that symbol with color(s). You can scribble if you want to.
3. Draw another large symbol to represent forgiveness. It may be the same symbol or a different one.
4. Write the person a letter inside the symbol telling them your feelings.
5. Draw one more symbol and color it in with an erasable pencil. Now find one point on it where you can imagine starting the forgiveness process and erase that little spot. In fact, erase as much as you want to.
6. Over the next week visualize releasing the anger and hurt. Erase a little more of the darkness in that circle of emotion.
7. View chains around that symbol. Each time you think of this you can erase more on your paper and visualize yourself breaking free from those emotional chains that used to bind you.
8. Now, draw and visualize bolt cutters severing that chain, which previously held you captive to shame, fear, and self-recrimination.
9. Draw the emotions flooding out.
10. Draw a beautiful scene, use colors that represent peace and growth. Inside the scene write the words, "The Wonder of Me." Fill in the paper with positive I am statements, A few ideas are:

> I AM PEACE
> I AM FORGIVENESS
> I AM LOVE
> I AM HOPE
> I AM LIGHT

11. Each time you think of and ask your Deity for help forgiving you can erase more.

12. Write what this process means to you. Discuss how forgiving someone can actually make you stronger and happier.

Footnote

1   Ten Boom, C. (2006). *The Hiding Place*. Grand Rapids, MI: Chosen Books.

Profile in Purpose & Valor – Connecting to the Courage Within

Purpose, Valor, Courage

Overcome your adversities,
Find a positive perspective in dire situations,
lean on those around you,
and find strength
in yourself and your community.
Johnny 'Joey' Jones

Odette Samson

Odette Samson was born in 1912 and died in 1995. She was a striking example of valor and courage. She married Roy Sansom in 1931 and they had three daughters before the beginning of World War II. In 1941 the English War Office asked for photographs of the coast of France. Odette had a few and sent them in, but to the wrong branch of the military. The Special Operations Executive saw the pictures and contacted her. They desperately needed women to work as spies, to return France and help England conquer the Nazis. She was, of course, hesitant to leave her family, but when she received word that her brother had been wounded in the war and her mother had to move because of the Nazis she decided to fight for England. The British military trained many agents to be put into France to spy to find out what the Germans were doing. This is her story, Pitogo, (2015)[1].

Odette went through basic training in England, then was transported to France by boat in October of 1942. Her code name was Lise, and she was a radio operator. The group she was placed in was headed by Peter Churchill, no relation to Winston Churchill. Being a "Radio Operator" was an extremely dangerous job because the Gestapo were constantly looking to intercept radio signals. She did this for a year before a double agent by the name of Colonel Henry reported her in April of 1943. (Odette Sansom Biography Online)[2].

Odette was taken to the Paris Fresnes Prison. She endured terrible interrogation and was tortured numerous times. She was beaten. They tore out her toenails and eventually even branded her spine with a hot iron. Still, she remained true to her story. She was adamant that she was the leader, not Peter Churchill. Despite the torture, she would not provide details on anyone else in her team. Finally, when they felt they could not get any more information from her she was sent to the Ravensbruck Concentration Camp to be executed. Do you remember her trainer, Peter Churchill? She refused to give them information on him, which made her torture worse. Yet, because they knew she was associated with him, it ironically saved her life. The Gestapo believed that she was related to Prime Minister Winston Churchill of the United Kingdom, this made her a bargaining chip.

The SS controlled her fate at the concentration camp. This group was Adolf Hitler's bodyguards and they grew to be the most feared and powerful of all organizations in Nazi Germany. They had sworn allegiance to Hitler and pledged their loyalty and ultimate obedience. If they did not obey, they could die. (History.Com Editors)[3].

In Ravensbruck Concentration Camp, Odette suffered more beatings and brutal treatment with long periods of solitary confinement. Finally, the prisoners were freed. Her war story was tragic as she had been betrayed by the double agent and captured by the Gestapo in France, sent to the Fresnes prison in France where she was tortured, then transported to the Ravensbrück where she endured more abuse and was starved. She emerged emaciated, weak, and gravely ill at the end of the war.

Despite her endured torture and trauma Ms. Sansom refused to be consumed with hatred. Instead, she used her energy to give service to charities by helping the victims of WWII. Basinger (2020)[4] reported on Sansom being awarded the George Cross, which was a very prestigious honor, but she only accepted it in honor of all agents who suffered in the war. She was noted as a woman who very well symbolized the great courage and invincible spirit of the fight against the Nazis and their philosophy of hatred.

Lesson

Odette Sansom was a woman of courage and honor. She was not a victim but a woman of courage. Her life became a light of hope to others maimed by war. In fact, she learned great truths from her experiences and wrote that suffering is part of life and that one should recognize that the battle against evil and hatred is never over but need not make a person live their life in negativity and resentment.

You have encountered many problems, some of which have taken courage to overcome. As you find your purpose in being, in the very premise of living you will also find rewards through added strength, focus, creativity, and expertise if you nurture that passion. For Odette, war forced her to redefine herself from being a mother and wife to also being a spy. She had to rely on her great belief in the ultimate goal, which was for the end of Nazism. Interestingly, this gave her added courage and stamina to withstand intense abuse.

You can imagine the prison where she was treated so cruelly, then the concentration camp. You can visualize the horrors of it, the barbed wire, the starving prisoners of war. Now, alter your focus to your place of peace, one you can return to repeatedly when you need to calm down and simply "be." One factor in finding one's purpose is to be able to get to that place of peace and tranquility by being one with it through visualization. This lesson's activity invites you to become the artist for your mental escape to the best place of peace for you.

> *When you spend as much time as I do with wounded warriors and their families, and terminally ill kids and their families, you are humbled and powerfully inspired by their courage and positive energy to live your life to the absolute best you can everyday. It will wake you up really fast to never stop believing.*
> **-Ted Nugent**

Activity

1. Design a place of peace rather than incarceration. What do you visualize as the antithesis or opposite of a prisoner of war camp?
2. Include art and athletic activities.
3. What type of food would you serve?
4. How would you make the surrounding area peaceful and beautiful?
5. Share your designs with class.

Footnotes

1   Pitogo, H. (2015, Mar 30). Odette Sansom, the First Woman to Receive the George Cross. War History Online. Retrieved from https://www.warhistoryonline.com/war-articles/wwii-stories-odette-sansom-the-first-woman-to-receive-the-george-cross.html

2   Odette Sansom Biography (n.d.) taken from Odette Hallowes, *The Times.* (17 March 1975). Found online 12/22/19 from https://www.biographyonline.net/military/odette-sanson.html

3   History.com Editors. (2009, Dec 18). The SS. https://www.history.com/topics/world-war-ii/ss

4   Basinger, R. (2020, May). Odette samson: The most decorated woman of world war ii. https://www.identifymedals.com/article/odette-sansom-the-most-decorated-woman-of-world-war-ii/ I.

Lesson 19

Kindness Overflowing

Remember there's no such thing
as a small act of kindness.
Every act creates a ripple with no logical end.
-Scott Adams

A Nurse Who Cared

The nurse received the beeping on her pager, she was part of the hospital's Rescue Team. She sprinted down the hallway to find a frail, elderly woman, shaking, eyes wide open with fear sitting in the hospital dining hall. Her skin was wrinkled, paper thin, and dirty white hair was plastered to her head. Her lips were cracked with dryness, her hands withered, and her wedding ring hung on a necklace, her final symbol of love and unity. She wore threadbare clothes with just a light sweater over a floral shirt. She was terrified. The crash cart was there, she was having chest pains and her temperature was low. The nurse, Christie, immediately took over care of Betty, this petite, frightened woman whose husband had died recently of a heart attack. Betty was tough and downplayed her symptoms, repeatedly stating that she did not want to bother anyone. Finally, she was lifted onto a trolley and wheeled down the hall with Christie reassuring her while holding her hand.[1]

Christie knew that nursing was and is a profession demanding time and energy and that sometimes the energy is depleted. She knew the fatigue of long hours of work and the weariness of tragedy. But Christie did not let any of that interfere with her care of Betty. She felt great empathy for the little woman and tucked the blanket around her as the bed moved through the hallways. She also tried to shield Betty from seeing traumatizing images of patients with gunshot or knife wounds. She was there to help and protect Betty.

Sitting and listening to someone is an act of compassion. Christie exemplified this, kindness flowed through her as she continued caring for the frail, sweet woman by finding her a heated blanket, and staying with her for as long as she could. She realized that Betty wasn't sick, she was grieving, lonely, cold, and afraid. Christy understood that Betty needed someone to take time with her, to listen to her story and let her life come to light with another person to witness. She needed to know that she still counted, that someone cared for her. Christie found that there was no family near her, no one to call to help or to visit so Christie remained by her side offering the gift of human kindness, which was the greatest of all gifts for Betty.

Christie understood the compassion needed if one chose to be an effective nurse, "Nursing requires fluidity, being able to adapt and push energy in the direction where patients and colleagues need you, even if it is unfamiliar," (Watson (2018, p. 26)[2].

Christie ended her story of Betty by writing, "...I stay another minute and close my eyes for a while and listen. Betty has a wonderful story. And if I listen hard enough, I stop seeing a frail old woman alone on a hospital trolley, and instead watch a young woman in a dress made from parachute silk dancing with her new husband, Stan," Watson (2018, p. 40)[3].

Lesson

To care for another person by offering a smile, a listening ear and an understanding heart is one of the greatest of gifts. This validates them and presents a message of courage, acceptance, and hope. Christie understood that being a nurse involved much more than medical care. An equally important aspect was compassion and empathy, and sometimes just to take time with a patient or family member. It is the initiative to step out of your own comfort zone and walk towards someone just to say hello and give them the opportunity to be heard.

You never know how powerful your influence can be. Stop and consider that sentence. Now determine right this moment to make your influence one that is positive, compassionate, and wise.

> *Guard well within yourself that treasure, kindness.*
> *Know how to give without hesitation,*
> *how to lose without regret,*
> *how to acquire without meanness.*
> **-George Sand**

Activity

1. What attributes did Christie have that made her a great nurse?
2. How did Christie know Betty was frightened?
3. Write an essay on the greatest act of kindness you have offered, or you have been given.
4. Share this with the class.
5. Discuss how the class can become a compassion-centered team.

Footnotes

1 Watson, C. (2018). *The language of kindness: A nurse's story.* NY: Tim Duggan Books.
2 Ibid.
3 Ibid.

Lesson 20

Mind-Body-Soul:
The Triad of Emotional Control

Highly sensitive people are too often perceived as weaklings or damaged goods. To feel intensely is not a symptom of weakness, it is the trademark of the truly alive and compassionate. It is not the empath who is broken, it is society that has become dysfunctional and emotionally disabled. There is no shame in expressing your authentic feelings. Those who are at times described as being a 'hot mess' or having 'too many issues' are the very fabric of what keeps the dream alive for a more caring, humane world. Never be ashamed to let your tears shine a light in this world.
— **Anthon St. Maarten**

The Prisoner

His name was Louis, known more widely as Louie. As a toddler he developed severe pneumonia, resulting in asthma so his parents moved to Torrance, California for the drier climate than what he had experienced in New York. They took the train, and as they left New York and slowly pulled out of Grand Central Station Louie jumped off the train and ran down the tracks. The conductor backed up the train to find him then his older brother, Pete, saw him calmly strolling up the track. When his mother picked him up, relief and love for her little boy flowed through her. He looked up and her and merely stated, "I knew you'd come back." Louie was two years old at the time! Hillenbrand (2010, p.)[1]

Louie was a challenge. His family was discriminated against because they were Italian. This was in the 1930s. As a child he stole food, would eat as much as he could, then toss the rest at people chasing him, store some, or give it away. He was constantly in trouble. Louie was small for his age and was often bullied until his father taught him how to defend himself, then he became the bully. He seemed to have no fears, except for flying. Throughout his youth and into the ninth grade Louie was out of control. His temper increased, his parents worried for his future, and his brother, Pete, tried to help. A few times even Pete was involved in Louie's pranks, but he never got caught because no one believed Pete would do anything wrong. The police visited the Zamperini home frequently, his father spanked Louie, the parents tried anything in an attempt to get him to behave, but nothing motivated a change in him. He seemed obsessed with destructive behaviors.

There was a new pseudoscience in America called eugenics. The movement was presented as a means of strengthening the human species, when in reality it was a study in horror, torture, and murder. A team of people decided to take or "cull" from humanity anyone they deemed as unworthy to be alive; the intellectually handicapped, which they labeled as feeble-minded, were targeted. They went after those they deemed as insane, others they focused on were criminals, women who had sex out of wedlock because eugenic authorities claimed it was a mental illness, orphans, anyone who was disabled, the homeless, poor, epileptics, the deaf, or the blind. Some advanced the idea of euthanasia, inaccurately named mercy killing, especially in mental hospitals where they would simply give a drug and kill any they judged to be unworthy to live. Another tactic was to sterilize anyone they felt should not procreate. Ultimately, there were twenty thousand people sterilized in California, Hillenbrand (2010)[2].

The year was 1931, Louie's criminal career had escalated, and his family was worried for his future, especially with the eugenics movement. His brother, Pete, intervened and convinced the school principal to let Louie be involved in athletics, the choice being track. Pete trained Louie relentlessly and although though Louie hated it, he feared the thought of eugenics more. Louie was finally motivated. He ran and ran and gave up drinking and smoking. He heard of Glenn Cunningham, a man who became his role model. When Glenn was young a fire killed his brother and severely burned Glenn to the point he had to relearn to walk, then committed himself to running, in 1932 becoming the greatest miler in America! (His story is also mentioned in Lesson 15).

Louie's running success suddenly made him popular, the girls swooned over him and he was elected class president. In 1933 he won the UCLA Cross Country two-mile race and did so by running a quarter mile ahead of the other runners. In 1936 he trained for the Olympics in Berlin and had multiple scholarships available to choose from. Louie, the boy who no one seemed to be able to control, who had no hope for a successful future, was now a leader, a winner in running, and heading to the Olympics. He didn't win but he did come in as the fastest 5000 sprinter, in 1936. Germany presented a united and kind front during the Olympics that year, however, after the banners disappeared the Nazi signs and flags were placed everywhere. The horrors of the World War II and Hitler's Regime were beginning in full force.

When Louie arrived home the town of Torrance held a parade in his honor. Louie and Pete looked forward to the Olympic games in 1940, where they felt Louie would be the winner, but world events changed. The war in Europe was raging so Louie joined the Air Corp to avoid being drafted. He did not want to go into the army, but he did not like flying, it still terrified him, so he did not complete his training. Then, an interesting thing happened, his discharge papers arrived but he disregarded them, and he was later drafted into the Air Force where he became one of the best bombadiers in his squadron, despite his fear of flying. In 1942 he graduated from Midland academy and was commissioned as a second lieutenant. His brother, Pete was a chief petty officer in the navy, Hillenbrand (2010)[3].

Life changed for everyone when Japan bombed Pearl Harbor. On August 19, 1942 Louie and his family gathered to have one more dinner together before Louie was sent to war. Louie was on the B-24 Liberator and he and a crew went out on a rescue mission in May of 1943. A plane had gone down, and they were searching for the pilot. Then, the horror happened, Louie's plane crashed into the ocean after a mechanical failure. There had been eleven men on board, only Louie, Russell Allen "Phil" Phillips and Francis "Mac" McNamara survived.

Imagine it! He, Phil, and Mac survived on a small raft, killing sharks as they circled them, while trying to find food. They had extremely limited quantities of water. One day an albatross landed on the raft and they considered eating it, but it smelled rotten. Later, another landed, which they killed and ate raw! Inside the bird were fish, which they then used for bait. The will to survive was strong. Their friend, Mac, died while they held him protectively in their arms. They had been on the raft thirty-four days. Louie and Phil eventually floated to shore, 2,000 miles from home on a Pacific Island, and they were taken as prisoners of war by the Japanese. (Biography.com editors, 2014)[4]. Louie and Phil and the other prisoners suffered horrible abuse. One camp commander, Mutsuhiro Watanabe, was brutal. The prisoners nicknamed him "the Bird" and he took it upon himself to torture Louie as much as he could, but Louie never let the man beat him spiritually or emotionally. Somehow, Louie and Phil and many others lived through starvation, insect infestations, beatings, and a variety of different types of torture. Louie's spunk and Phil's great courage helped them fight through to the end of the war.

On August 15, 1945 Japanese Emperor Hirohito announced the surrender of Japan, the document was officially signed on September 2, 1945. However, on August 22nd the camp commander walked into the barracks, approached the ranking American officer, Lieutenant Colonel Marion Unruh, and stated, "the emperor has brought peace to the world!" (Hillenbrand, 2010, p. 308)[5]. The reality was that Japan had surrendered.

Finally, the war was over, Louie, Phil, and other POWs were released. It was glorious and tragic. Seeing the devastation their bodies were in, hearing of what they had endured was heart-wrenching, but they had survived. Louie returned home, married, and was eager to start a new life, but the horrors of war, the nightmares, and what we now call Post Traumatic Stress Disorder (PTSD), then referred to as combat fatigue, or battle fatigue, were consuming him. He turned to alcohol to sleep, numb the pain, and to survive the memories, which were so vivid in his mind. It was destroying him and his marriage.

The marriage suffered. Louie simply could not be there emotionally for his wife. One night his wife attended a local rally, it was a revival meeting and Billy Graham, the evangelist, was speaking. She felt touched by his message and began to have hope, then she finally convinced Louie to attend a meeting. He went once, she begged him to go again, hoping and praying he would open his heart to the message. Reverend Graham spoke of the atrocities of war and asked how a caring God could allow it to happen, then he offered a powerful message on how God did reach out by giving people the strength to endure hardships.

During the meeting, Louie remembered their raft being riddled with bullets, but also recognized that none hit him, Mac, or Phil. Louie started to panic, he raced for the door, but a miracle happened. Everything around him seemed to disappear and he was lost in the memory of being back on the raft hearing the promise he had made to God, "…if you will save me, I will serve you forever" Hillenbrand (2010, p. 375)[6].

That moment became monumental in his life, it was the last flashback he ever had. When he got home, he went to the liquor cabinet and threw all the alcohol out and began a life of service. He was finally at peace. He toured the country speaking about the war and the importance of faith. Eventually, he set up the nonprofit Victory Boys Camp where he took in any wayward youth and taught them how to live life, and face challenges by taking them hiking, rock climbing, swimming, boating, horseback riding and skiing in the winters, Hillenbrand (2010)[7]. Louie had found peace, "When he thought of his history, what resonated with him now was not all that he had suffered but the divine love that he believed had intervened to save him. He was not the worthless, broken, forsaken man that the Bird had striven to make of him. In a single, silent moment, his rage, fear, humiliation, and sense of helplessness, had fallen away. That morning, he believed, he was a new creation…softly, he wept." (Hillenbrand, 2010, p. 376).[8]

This is the history of Louie Zamperini. Laura Hillenbrand gave his story added awareness in her book, *Unbroken,* which later became a movie.

> *How can you tell of being victimized by such*
> *monstrous men, yet not express rage?*
> *His response was simple: Because I forgave them."*
> **Louie Zamperini**

Lesson

Louie had to learn to control his emotions before he could control his life. He chose to replace alcohol with his new-found faith in God to help him get through each day. His faith and commitment to sobriety helped propel him to a life of service. Thoughts and emotions interact, one is not present without the other. This brings into play the critical importance of emotional intelligence, which involves one's perceptions of themselves and their lives and history and how their emotions affect their decision making, understanding and regulation of emotion so that others are not "harmed," (Mayer, Salovery, & Caruso, 2004).[9]

Schutte, et al. (2006) reported that the effective use of emotions increases the spiritual depth of human relationships, the ability to handle stress more effectively, and improve problem solving skills. As you develop greater awareness of self and others you increase your ability to have accurate perceptions of people and events. This is so exciting because your understanding of situations and people is heightened, which helps you to manage yours and other's emotions with more calmness and clarity. The added benefit is lowered levels of anxiety and depression! Research shows that when you develop more consistent and healthy emotional intelligence you are more apt to be optimistic and recover from negative situations, which adds to your overall health, (Schutte, Malouff, Sminuek, Hollander, & McKenley, 2002).[10]

Mayer and Salovey offered their own definition of emotional intelligence as "...the ability to monitor one's own and others' feelings and emotions, to discriminate among them and to use their information to guide one's thinking and actions," (Bariso, 2018, p. 8)[11]. Sharma, Mishra, and Sharma (2014)[12] stated that the importance of emotional intelligence is having "...the ability to recognize different feelings emanating from within and giving a name to them." (p. 126). The key idea is for each of us to recognize our emotions, be able to label them, process, control, and point them into a positive direction. When one can control their responses, they are the one whom people will trust to honor themselves and others and to offer pro-social solutions and ideas.

Daniel Goleman (1998)[13] presented a five-dimension model to discern one's emotional intelligence.

Self-Awareness: This is a person's ability to recognize, judge, and truly be aware of a feeling. It includes confidence and self-assessment in that process.

Self-Management: Every person has points of sensitivity and some will react, rather than calmly assess the situation and the emotion. The ability to exert self-control over impulsive emotions, thoughts and actions is critical for self-management. It invites integrity, patience, adaptability, and personal responsibility.

Motivation: When a person is in control of his/her emotions they can help empower others, be part of goalsetting, and achievement. Motivation's big helpers are optimism, self-confidence, commitment, and personal initiative.

Empathy: The person who is empathetic understands someone else's emotions and they are sensitive to those. Instead of reacting to them, even if the other person is angry, it is the strength of character that allows the individual to step back and look at the source of the emotion, which might be fear, anxiety, depression, frustration, a feeling of abandonment or vulnerability, etc.

Social Skills: The ability to get along with others, to engage in conversations and be a source of positive messages and understanding is part of the social skills needed for emotional intelligence. The other aspect includes positive leadership and the ability to cooperate and work in a team or group setting.

When you control your emotions, you control your life. The following activity is designed to assist you in realizing the power of emotions.

Activity

1. If Louie were a child now, how do you think he would have been treated in the educational, law enforcement, and medical system?
2. Who and what guided him to find a purpose?
3. How did his personal character strengths help him survive the concentration camps?
4. What happened in his mind to heal him so that he could quit drinking and become a great success?
5. This is a team activity. Being in-tune with your emotions allows you internal control to move towards your dreams. This week's activity is focused on where you are living right now. Using the five dimensions of emotional intelligence listed above, take one aspect of the facility rules where you are currently living and determine how these fit into each other.

What is your primary problem with your setting?	What is a viable solution?
Self-Awareness	How does this impact you?
Self-Awareness	How can you make this positive?
Self-Management	What can you do differently to help yourself and others?

Self-Management	What areas do you need to exert more patience and self-control?
Motivation	What positive emotions and behaviors can you adopt to create a healthier environment?
Empathy	Think of the other's perspective. What can you learn about them to bring understanding to you?
Social Skills	How can you as a class be a "team" to help each other to make positive, kind, and success-oriented decisions?

Footnotes

1   Hillenbrand, L. (2010). *Unbroken*. NY: Random House.

2   Ibid.

3   Ibid.

4   Biography.com Editors. (20 August, 2019). Louis Zamperini biography.

5   Hillenbrand, L. (2010). *Unbroken*. NY: Random House.

6   Ibid.

7   Ibid.

8   Ibid.

9   Mayer, J. D., Salovey, P., & Caruso, D. (2004). Emotional intelligence: theory, findings, and implications. *Psychological Inquiry*, 15, 197–215

10 Schutte, N. S., Malouff, J. M. Thorsteinsson, E. B. Bhullar, N., and Rooke, S. E. (11 October 2006). A meta-analytic investigation of the relationship between emotional intelligence and health Personality and Individual Differences 42 (2007) 921–933. Retrieved from ScienceDirect.com (https://www.researchgate.net/profile/Einar_Thorsteinsson/publication/216626194_A_metaanalytic_investigation_of_the_relationship_between_emotional_intelligence_and_health/links/5b1793...) February 26, 2020.

11   Bariso, J. (2018). EQ Applied: The Real World Guide to Emotional Intelligence. Germany: Borough Hall.

12   Sharma, D., Mishra, I. and Sharma, M.V. (2014). Emotional intelligence among employees of government and public sectors. *International Journal of Social Sciences. Vol. 3* (3).

13   Goleman, D. (1998). Working with Emotional Intelligence 10. Goleman, D. (2006), Social Intelligence: The New Science of Human Relationships

Difficult Conversations: Learning to Listen, Learning to Share

You can talk with someone for years, everyday, and still,
it won't mean as much as what you can have
when you sit in front of someone,
not saying a word,
yet you feel that person with your heart,
you feel like you have known the person for forever
...connections made with the heart...not the tongue.
C. Joy Bell

Service: A Window of Opportunity

Daniel was fifteen, angry, and defiant. He was lost, no real group of friends seemed to fulfill his search for identity and meaning in life. He was leery of anyone trying to help him. In fact, anytime a teacher called on him or anyone called him to the office he assumed he was in trouble and his defenses rose to the point that he was belligerent and hostile. The school counselor simply waited and watched, smiling at the young man, asking him to sit down and relax. "You aren't in trouble. I simply want to meet you and ask you if you are interested in a program we are running. I am looking for student leaders to be trained to help out in the community."

Daniel was astonished. Why would anyone want his help? What was the angle? "Why, why are you asking me?" he questioned the counselor, again with hostility, but the counselor maintained her control and kindness and just said, "I've been watching you, Dan. In you, I see hope and courage. I know you have been through a lot and because of that you will be able to understand the pain others carry, perhaps more than some students would."

Finally, he let down his guard. "Tell me more about it," he muttered. After their discussion he agreed to give it a try. He knew he would have to clean up, look sharp, and learn what he was going to help with, and that was exciting to him. For the first time he felt noticed and challenged.

For the next several months he got trained in peer tutoring and helping younger children learn to read. At the end he received a certificate of accomplishment. It was a turning point in his life and from there he went to high school, could works towards a scholarship, and pursue his dreams.

Now let us turn back the pages of time and review more significant facts about Daniel. He had moved to a new neighborhood, did not know anyone, and eventually the taunts of other students and the abandonment of his father weighed heavily upon him. He started sluffing, getting in trouble, and engaging in some vandalism. His mother loved him, but she was stretched to the limit caring for the other children and putting food on the table.

Daniel was at a crossroads, and he seemed to recognize it. He needed something to change and he really did want to succeed, so the counselor's offer to be in the peer training and leadership group was exactly what he needed, and which gave him purpose and enthusiasm. Service is magical. The more a person forgets themselves and serves others the greater the opportunities for personal fulfillment occur.

Lesson

The title of this lesson is *Difficult Conversations*. Daniel was used to being on his own, his family was scattered, and he had not learned effective communication. In the story the counselor found it difficult to set a dress code for Daniel, but the service she was inviting him to participate in was one where a neat and clean appearance was important. She gave Daniel the choice and he was the one to accept the challenge and glory in the work.

Prior to this, Daniel faced a lot of challenges in trying to fit into a new neighborhood and school, being bullied, and getting into trouble with the police. Taking care of his appearance was not a priority and his depression added to his reticence to clean up more. Even though his home life was chaotic however, he did have the consistent love from his mother. He approached the counselor with a sense of dread, born out of fear. The fear led him to having a hostile attitude. Then, the wonder of kindness happened when the counselor looked behind the mask and saw a troubled young man desperately wanting to fit in. He was smart, feisty, and determined. She wanted to harness those energies and direct them to a positive endeavor. When the peer leadership program began, she thought of Daniel and interviewed him.

The circle below with the list of words and the chart demonstrate the power of hurtful emotions. Daniel experienced all of these. The counselor took the time to teach him to step out of the circle of emotion and into the world of hope. "Daniel, that pit of anger, hopelessness, and hatred is dark and consuming. You will never find happiness there." She taught Daniel and the other students important visualizing and calming techniques, the health benefits of music, art, writing, talking, and serving others. Slowly, Daniel began to feel that he belonged, he had new friends, a purpose, and all aspects of his life improved. He also recognized that he needed to learn to love and accept himself.

All of us have feelings of inadequacy and fear. Daniel's issues of abandonment and anger were significant. The counselor saw that if he continued to stay on the path he was currently entrenched in, he would have trouble completing high school and staying out of trouble. He had suffered a lot in his youth, which of course carried over into adolescence and adulthood. But he also had a dream of living a better life and was smart enough to grab hold of the opportunity and let it consume him. He learned tools for successful communication which helped him continue in his schooling.

Effective and open communication can bring a healthy balance into the communication dyad. It is a complex process requiring thought, patience, creativity, empathy, and compassion. If we view it in terms of conversations, we can go through, think about, and discuss each of these steps to best ensure that the communication and conversation will have a positive outcome.

Listen with curiosity. Speak with honesty. Act with integrity.
The greatest problem with communication is we don't listen to understand.
We listen to reply.
When we listen with curiosity, we don't listen with the intent to reply.
We listen for what's behind the words.
- Roy T. Bennett. The Light in the Heart.

1. Is this conversation necessary?
2. Is this the right time to talk with the person?
3. Am I calm and able to discuss my feelings without bringing harm to the relationship or hurting them?
4. How will I know if I have said enough?
5. How can I best say it, with tact, and without cruel intent?
6. Am I able to sit and listen with my heart, mind, ears, eyes, and soul?
7. Timing is critical. Being tactful is necessary. The dosage is the clincher.

Activity

1. Write or discuss a conversation that did not turn out well. Look at your own role in it and contemplate what you could have done

better. Also, what could the other person have said to help the situation remain calm and less heated?

2. As a class think of the main character in a movie where there was an argument. Discuss the following:

What was the argument about?

Was fear a primary factor?

How was disrespect shown?

Was the discussion necessary? If so, how could it have been handled better?

Was the timing right for finding solutions?

How was the topic presented, with hostility and anger or calmly?

What were the body language indicators for both people?

Stance

Tone of Voice

What language was used

Was the voice loud or soft

Was one person more volatile than the other

Position of hands

Position of arms

Position of legs

Movement of hands, arms, legs

Where was the person looking

Who was showing the most personal restraint

What positive things occurred, if any

What did you learn about each person by observing their interaction

Lesson 22

The Gift of Empathy

You can only understand people if you feel them in yourself.
– John Steinbeck

Mayor Fiorello LaGuardia

It was a cold winter day. Many people were starving and did not have enough clothing or shelter. A police officer walked into the court room, ushering a shabbily clothed man. The man looked defeated and distraught. The mayor wondered what this man could have done. When the story unfolded the lesson began. "Sir, this man is charged with stealing a loaf of bread." The defendant tearfully told his story. His family was starving, his children crying. He had to feed them, so he went out to find them food. He saw a loaf of bread and stole it, not for himself, but his family. The man was afraid, appearing before New York's Mayor, Fiorello LaGuardia, who also presided over the police court. It was the era of the "great depression" 1934-1939, and millions were starving. Here stood a man poorly dressed and without hope, standing there humbly waiting for his sentence, wondering if he would be thrown in jail. (Fadiman, 1985)[1].

The mayor was in a bind. The man had broken the law, but he understood why. Finally, the mayor declared, "The fine will be 10 dollars." The man was astonished. He did not have a penny! How could he possibly pay a ten-dollar fine? In a split second he pictured himself thrown in jail and his family completely abandoned, but then a miracle happened. The mayor stated, "Here's the 10 dollars to pay your fine," and he pulled the money from his own pocket and gave it to the man. Then, Mayor LaGuardia looked out over the courtroom and declared, "I'm going to fine everybody here 50 cents for living in a town where a man has to steal bread to eat." The order was given, the Bailiff collected the money from everyone and gave it to the man, who was absolutely stunned. He left the courtroom with $47.50! Everyone in attendance received a powerful lesson in mercy and empathy (Fadiman 1985, p. 339)[2].

Lesson

There is a famous musical called Les Miserable, written from the text of the book with the same name, by Victor Hugo. The main character, Jean Valjean, was arrested for stealing a loaf of bread, similar to the story above. There are different reasons one would steal, most are for money or sources of material to buy drugs, and most are definitely illegal acts. For someone to steal a loaf of bread to feed a starving family reaches into the greatest depths of humanity. In a perfect society no one would be hungry, those with money would help those in need. This is seen daily with billions of dollars being disseminated to help the needy. And, in turn, the needy can, where possible, give back by working or providing service to another.

Empathy is the great ability to "walk in another's shoes" for a moment in time. It is the willingness to tune into one's soulfulness and ask, how can I better understand this person so that I can actually help them? Sometimes it is simply the ability and willingness to listen and offer a word of encouragement. Empathy and kindness go hand in hand. There are occasions where it is difficult to understand another's motive. When a parent strikes a child or a child bullies another it is hard to find empathy for the aggressor. Sometimes, though, the bully at school is the one being beaten at home, understanding that opens the pathway to finding help for the bully and providing comfort to the victim.

Activities

1. Draw a pair of shoes of someone you know has been hurt but they take it out on others.
2. Tune into their reasons for acting out. Use colors to represent their pain and anger.
3. Write a paragraph on why you think they would act the way they do.
4. Imagine yourself in their shoes. What pain can you connect with?
5. Write a paragraph about an experience in your life when you just needed someone to understand what you were going through.
6. Discuss this as a class and each person is invited to share one experience when they did feel empathy for another.
7. As a class review the chart of empathy.

Empathy is about standing in someone else's shoes,
feeling his or her heart,
seeing with his or her eyes.
Not only is empathy hard to outsource and automate,
but it makes the world a better place.
Daniel Pink

Chart: Questions About Empathy

Empathy Blockers	Empathy Embracers
Was I cruel?	Did I stop to think how my actions affected them, why they reacted negatively?
Did I intimidate?	Did I speak to them on their level, with respect?
Was I judgmental in my assessment?	Was I fair and reasonable in my assessment?
Did selfishness rule my decision?	Was I selfless in seeking a solution?

Did I bring harm to the relationship?	Was I kind?
Did I assume?	Did I seek knowledge before making a decision?
Did I dismiss their feelings?	Did I consider their feelings?
Did I let the other person's reaction determine my reaction?	Did I dismiss the other person's emotional reaction and allow myself time to think through the problem logically?
Did I manipulate to get something from them?	Was I sincere in my interest in them, my concern for their well-being?
Did I consider the consequences of what I said or did?	Was I considerate of their feelings and the long-term ramifications of my intended comments or actions?
Did I expect them to forgive me even though I had forgiven them?	Did I consider that forgiveness is on a timeline and that I cannot demand that of others?
Did I hold a grudge and let the anger fester?	Did I seek help to learn how to let the issue go, and realize that it takes time to get over emotional and physical wounds?
Did I tell them I was sorry or just expect them to know that?	Did I invite the other person to greater healing and understanding through my apology?
Did I choose to continue in my thoughts, emotions, and actions?	Did I choose to commit to self-change and do whatever it took to make those changes?

Footnote

1 Fadiman, C. (Ed.). (1985). *The little brown book of anecdotes.* NY: Hatchette Book Group.
2 Ibid.

Lesson 23

Respond, Don't React

People aren't just ants rushing around over a crust of bread. Every life, no matter how isolated, touches hundreds of others. It's up to us to decide if those micro connections are positive or negative. But whichever we decide, it does impact the ones we deal with. One word can give someone the strength they needed at that moment or it can shred them down to nothing. A single smile can turn a bad moment good. And one wrong outburst or word could be the tiny push that causes someone to slip over the edge into destruction.
-Sherrilyn Kenyon

When Conflict Arises

What do you do when conflict arises? Are you one who can respond or one who reacts. Let's take a situation where you are at work. The phone rings and you are called to the office. You pick up the receiver and someone just starts yelling at you. Here is a critical point. Are you going to hang up? Yell back at the person? Cry? Swear? Walk away? Wait until the rant I over and you can then have your voice? When situations like this arise, there is always the choice. The most helpful thing is to make the choice beforehand. That means, cultivating seeds of peace within your soul. When you choose to be a peacemaker you are honoring your own integrity and soulfulness. Soulfulness is the ability to express feelings tender and spiritual in depth. We each have darkness and we each have light. Thomas Moore (2004) wrote, "AT ONE TIME or another, most people go through a period of sadness, trial, loss, frustration, or failure that is so disturbing and long-lasting that it can be called a dark night of the soul. If your main interest in life is health, you may quickly try to overcome the darkness. But if you are looking for meaning, character, and personal substance, you may discover that a dark night has many important gifts for you." Moore (2004, loc 111)[1].

Each of us has those dark nights, times we may feel unsure, hard to love, vulnerable, and sad. For others it moves into depression that is so significant it pulls energy from the individual and lessens productivity. However, if we take the time to look at the sadness, anger, disappointment, and frustration, and allow ourselves to experience it, then visualize it flowing through us and leaving, releasing from our mind and body, we will learn pearls of wisdom to glean from it. This requires a degree of optimism, which is a positive view of present and future. When an individual embraces an attitude of positive alternatives it creates a movement of energy, one catapulting the person onto a platform of positive self-regard, joy in life, and improved mental wellness. This, then, generalizes to enhanced self-efficacy and confidence.

Dr. Martin Seligman (2006)[2] provided the P.E.R.M.A. model, five components that can be adapted to one's character and help them dream big dreams, set realistic goals, and find optimism in the process. These are provided online @ (Http://www.gostrengths.com/whatisperma/)

- **P**ositive emotions – feeling good
- **E**ngagement – being completely absorbed in activities
- **R**elationships – being authentically connected to others
- **M**eaning – purposeful existence
- **A**chievement – a sense of accomplishment and success

To respond vs. react invites the participant into the world of imagination, creativity, self-control, and delayed gratification of needs. When a peaceful solution is reached each person can feel better about themselves and one another. There is a sense of achievement and well-being. Now let's return to the store managers problem. He finally receives a very kind and understanding letter from president of the corporation. They, too, had lost power, many goods were damaged, there was civil unrest, and they were trying very hard to get help to him. The president also stated that his mail had been stolen so had had just recently retrieved the letter. Using the following rubric walk through any problem you are having with someone else. Learning to respond and not react to respond and not react requires self-discipline, patience, and commitment. An excellent example of the "Respond Don't React" Model is provided below. Read the following case example and picture the scenario and your own thoughts on the situation.

Respond or React
Emotion-Laden Critical Thinking Analysis

	Case Example	Relevancy
Initial Incident Becoming aware of the needs of others and self.	The manager was concerned about their department and employees, they were out of food and supplies. The manager was afraid some would perish.	When have you seen a need in another person and tried to find a way to help them?

Communication Dimensions:	The manager wrote to the president of the company asking for supplies. But in the letter, the manager severely criticized the president for not doing anything to help them. The assumption was made that the president was hoarding all the supplies, food, and money.	When have you not had the correct information or knowledge that someone did need help?
Understand the problem. Consider long-term ramifications. Controlling emotions and not over-reacting. Willingness to LISTEN and LEARN		When have you felt verbally assaulted but refused to react? Instead, you responded with rational, calm thought and communication. Or, when is a time you reacted irrationally and what could you have done differently?
	The president read the letter and felt great concern and sorrow for the manager's department. The president wrote back that the whole company was suffering, and low supplies were an issue due to a hurricane. Phone lines were down, computers were not functioning, everything was chaotic, the president was worried about his employees. The president responded with a heart-felt letter.	When have you noticed that family or friends needed help and you had misunderstood the situation, and assumed the worst?

Character Building		
F.A.I.T.H. Model Faith – Faith in fellow human Faith in the higher power - Faith in "the universe" Adaptability – Ability to adapt to different circumstances Integrity – Honesty Trustworthy - Honorable Hope – Positive expectations	Once they had communicated, both the manager and the president were unitedly concerned about their employees and communities. They treated the employees with respect and worked right beside them. The manager and president encouraged the employees in their goals at home and work. They believed in the company mission and in the individual. Each employee went the extra mile because they respected and honored their leaders. The employees trusted them and found hope in serving the greater good with the company.	How can you allow time to wait to find out the whole story before jumping to conclusions? How can you be an example of the F.A.I.T.H. Model? Provide a specific example of a time you showed: • Faith • Adaptability • Integrity • Trustworthiness • Hope

Lesson

The case study of the manager and the president presented here opens your mind to how we can make assumptions and jump to the wrong conclusions. By not being humble and willing to seek more information we can make serious mistakes even when we are doing so for the right reasons. The manager was a tremendous leader and honored his employees. The president was also a great leader, respecting her employees and their families. There were no phones or means of communication during the hurricane and other storm in the small village. As the story unfolded you saw how concerned both were, how the manager wrote for help, explaining his situation, then how it escalated to anger and erroneous assumptions. The president did not take offense, instead, she had strengthened her character through years of kindness, service, and integrity. She was a woman of compassion and goodness. As soon as she had the correct information, she worked to correct the problem and provide helpful information rather react with an angry retort. This is a lesson for each of us to stop, think, gather facts, and ponder on the best, healthiest, most peaceful solutions.

Activity

1. Answer the questions in the rubric.
2. Discuss someone who is an example of the FAITH model.
3. Discuss how you can offer healthy solutions to others.

**Stop and think, for as you allow a moment to
clear your head and open your heart
you will invite the spirit of peace, empathy, and wisdom.
-Jan C. Booth**

**All battles are first won or lost, in the mind.
-Joan of Arc**

Footnote

1   Moore, T. (2004). Dark nights of the soul. NY: Penguin Publishing Group. Kindle Edition.
2   Seligman, M. E. (2006). Learned optimism. New York, NY: Bantam Books.

Lesson 24

Family and Community Support Can Light the Flame of Hope

You must never look for a reason to help those who yearn for support.
Extending a helping hand not only vanishes tears off their face,
but also act as a cure for oneself.
-Prachi Paktar

Diagnosis

The man faced a critical moment, his pain, was intense, the doctor did an ultrasound and found a large tumor on his bladder. The same week he received his diagnosis of an inoperable tumor he and his wife discovered they were going to have a child. The biopsy had to be done but led to a complication, an infection that resulted in gangrene. He was given about a 5% chance to live if he went into a barometric chamber where pure oxygen would be pumped into his stomach to kill the bacteria. His reply was to do it, he was determined to live. His will to survive was unconquerable. He told the doctors to do whatever it took to keep him alive until his child was born and to use his body for science in trying to find a cure for cancer.

The next few months were horrific! Pain, side effects from chemo and radiation, and reactions to the multiple drugs he was given were terrible to deal with, but he did not give up. The family and community rallied around him and helped his wife. A new roof was put on their home at no cost, meals were taken in, money donated, nothing was too great of a task to offer this small family.

The months seemed to pass quickly, he grew thinner and gaunt, a mere shadow of the man he used to be, but his spirit remained strong. Finally, the day of delivery came, his wife was on one floor of the hospital, he on another. He gradually got himself off the bed and worked his way down to comfort his wife and meet his new baby. There he was grinning, weeping with joy and love beyond which words can tell. He had his IV pole with him, he was dressed in a hospital gown and robe, but none of that mattered. He was where he wanted to be, one with wife, and newborn son and his two-year-old boy.

The father died a few weeks later, but he had achieved his dream of meeting his child and being there for his beloved wife. His wife continued raising her children, a woman of honor, determination, and endurance. She kept a sense of humor, she viewed life through an introspective wide-angle lens realizing that even though tragedy happens there is a reason for everything. She became an anchor of faith and strength to others and continued exemplifying compassion, persistence, love, and loyalty throughout her life, and continues to do so, many years later. This is a story of courage, a story of love, and a story of commitment. It is a tribute to a woman who is, indeed, a fountain of joy and love to her family and to all she meets.

Lesson:

This is a true story of the power of love, the importance of family, and the compassion and service that community can offer. The truth is that when you open your heart to others you are inviting miracles, you become the catalyst to bringing hope to the wounded soul.

For a moment, consider the wife. She was faced with a major crisis, dealing with pregnancy, chasing an 18-month-old child around, visiting the hospital, keeping the home as calm as possible, relying on family and friends to tend, and adjusting to the awareness of probably losing her husband. Throughout those months and ensuing years, she faced heartache, profound grief, and uncertainty about her future and being able to provide for her family. Still, as previously stated and now repeated for emphasis, she remained a woman of faith, hope, kindness, humor, and love.

Assignment:

1. As a class organize a community project that will benefit others.
2. Select the population you want to help.
3. Each member of the class will decide what skill they can bring to the effort.
4. Write up a viable plan.
5. Discuss this in class.

Lesson 25

When You Are Thrown A Curve Simply Dig Deeper to Accomplish Your Goals

Laughter is timeless,
imagination has no age
and dreams are forever.
Walt Disney

From Mickey to A World of Fascination

Walter Elias Disney was born in Chicago, Illinois on December 5, 1901 to Elias and Flora Disney. He had three brothers and one sister. At the age of four, Walt moved with his family to a farm in Marceline, Illinois. His love for drawing was launched when his neighbor, Doc Sherwood, asked him to sketch his horse, Rupert. He even paid Walt for the drawing and this sparked his imagination. He loved drawing, trains fascinated him, and when he was old enough, he sold popcorn, sodas, and newspapers to people traveling through.

When Walt was ten, the family moved again, this time to Kansas City where he and his sister, Ruth, went to the Benton Grammar School, and on Saturdays he took courses at the Kansas City Art Institute. He and his sister would frequent the Electric Park, which not only captivated him, but influenced his later designs for Disneyland. Then, in 1917 his family moved to Chicago. Walt was then a freshman at McKinley High School, and he kept up his art training by taking night classes at the Chicago Art Institute. During high school he started doing drawings for the school newspaper.

Walt surprised his family by dropping out of high school when he was 16 to enlist in the army, but was too young, so he joined the Red Cross and was sent to France where he was assigned to be an ambulance driver. He covered the ambulance with drawings of cartoon characters! (Lad, 2019)[1].

Walt continued drawing, then in 1948 wrote an essay titled "What Mickey Mouse Means to Me." The birth of Mickey was a result of a major crisis in Walt's life. He and his brother Roy were busy with Walt's successful cartoon character, Oswald the Lucky Rabbit who was suddenly stolen by the Universal distributor Charles Mintz. He also took many of Walt's artists. This was an economic blow and an artistic one, but suddenly Walt had the idea of a little mouse, which his mother named Mickey![2] His first completed Mickey cartoon was called *Plane Crazy*, inspired by the first solo flight across the Atlantic Ocean by Charles Lindbergh. The cartoon included Mickey and friends trying to build their own plane and premiered in Hollywood on May 1, 1928. It was rejected and he could not find anyone to distribute it so he created *The Gallopin' Gaucho*, which was also rejected. Walt didn't let those setbacks defeat him. He continued to work on his little mouse and came up with *Steamboat Willie* on November 18, 1928. This aired in New York's Colony Theatre and was a big success. It was also one of the first cartoons to link with synchronized sound. Walt received $1,000.00 for the two-week run of the cartoon. This was an enormous sum to be paid for a cartoon on Broadway.

We all have et backs and another one for Walt was with his first animation studio, which was called "Laugh-o-Gram." This told modernized versions of fairy tales based on Aesop's Fables. The venture quickly went bankrupt, noted Spiegel (2020)[2].

Several dates were given for the "birth" of Mickey Mouse but the final one decided upon was November 18, 1928, which was also the birth of Minnie Mouse, known in the Steamboat Willie cartoon as the little female mouse running along the riverbank to catch "Pegleg Pete's" steamboat. Walt Disney had the ability to spark the child within with his cartoons, animated movies, and other movies of lasting impression such as *Pollyanna, Old Yeller, Treasure Island, The Shaggy Dog, Pollyanna, Swiss Family Robinson, The Absent Minded Professor, Mary Poppins,* and more. His amusement parks provide entry into the world of imagination and creativity and his dream of bringing joy to every child was certainly fulfilled, Gluck (2011)[3].

Lesson

Often, we assume that an artist starts out at the level of drawing we view and forget that the artist had a starting point and worked and studied diligently to get to the point of producing great works of art. Walt Disney never gave up. He started drawing around the age of four and continued throughout his life. He had high standards for his employees and his legend remains one of lasting joy through the annals of time. He embraced life with joy, had his own struggles, but refused to give up. Instead, his life is a legacy of joy and fun, and most of all memories of shared wonder.

Activity

1. Draw a cartoon image of anything you want.
2. Make a cartoon strip out of it with a positive message.
3. Share with the class.

Cartoon Construct

Name of Cartoon Strip

Characters

Theme

Footnotes

1   Lad, K. (26 March, 2019). Undeniably Interesting Facts about Walt Disney's Childhood. Retrieved from https://entertainism.com/walt-disneys-childhood

2   Spiegel, R. (2020). 46 magical facts about walt Disney. https://www.factinate.com/people/46-magical-facts-walt   Disney/#:~:text=Walt%Disney%20 Facts.

3   Gluck, Keith. (18 November 2011). The Birth of a Mouse. The Walt Disney Family Museum (2018). Retrieved from https://www.waltdisney.org/blog/birth-mouse

Lesson 26

Just Breathe

In a quiet place, close your eyes, take a deep breath, and go inward.
Place your attention on your heart, in the center of your chest.
Sit quietly and easily let your attention remain there.
-Deepak Chopra

Buzz Aldrin

The year was 1969, the Apollo 11 mission to the moon commenced through the intricately designed and intense rocket launchers. Neil Armstrong, Michael Collins, and Buzz Aldrin made up the team. When the five Saturn rockets launched as the most powerful engines in the world, they accelerated to new velocities. The forces and massive power were extraordinary. The medical team in Houston monitored the heart rates of the three astronauts. At launch, Michael Collins heart rate was 99 beats per minutes and Neil Armstrong's was 110 bpm, Buzz Aldrin's was 88 bpm. When Neil and Buzz descended the spacecraft to walk on the moon, their heart rates were still monitored. In the final parts of the descent, Buzz was calling reporting on the sparsity of fuel, but there was still 20 seconds left until landing. If the fuel got to zero, they would have to abort the landing. Fortunately, they made it and the two men were the first humans to step foot on the moon. By the time they stepped out onto the lunar surface Neil's heart rate went up to 114 bpm, and Buzz's heart rate was 81 bpm. He had an ability to remain calm even in the face of this potential crisis, Verger (2019)[1]. Neil was the first to walk on the moon, however, Buzz Aldrin joined him, where they studied the surface and other factors of the moon then returned to earth with no problems. It was a time that brought new meaning to life on our planet and to the world beyond.

Lesson

The research on being able to stop and breathe slowly is astounding. Buzz Aldrin had the ability to stay calm in the face of danger. Buzz believed in gaining as much knowledge as possible and having an awareness of the past is part of that. He said, "Knowledge of the past and an optimistic view of the present give you great opportunities." https://thedecalife.com/top-10-buzz-aldrin-quotes/

So often we have a tendency to dwell on the past, but the question becomes, how can you learn from your life experiences and use them to move forward instead of backwards? What new knowledge do you need to help you? Buzz refused to view failure as a stopping point, "Some people don't like to admit that they have failed or that they have not yet achieved their goals or lived up to their own expectations. But failure is not a sign of weakness. It is a sign that you are alive and growing. (https://thedecalife.com/top-10-buzz-aldrin-quotes/). His life lessons are provided eloquently in his own words.

These are a few of my favorite life lessons that I learned as a result of walking on the Moon and the preparation that took us there and the guiding principles that have helped keep me going since returning to Earth: The sky is not the limit ... there are footprints on the Moon! Keep your mind open to possibilities. Show me your friends, and I will show you your future. Second comes right after first. Write your own epitaph. Maintain your spirit of adventure. Failure is always an option. Practice respect for all people. Do what you believe is right even when others choose otherwise. Trust your gut ...

and your instruments. Laugh … a lot! Keep a young mind-set at every age. Help others go beyond where you have gone. (https://thedecalife.com/top-10-buzz-aldrin-quotes/)

Learning to remain calm in the face of adversity is a skill that will help you throughout your life. Your brain is used to living one way, oftentimes causing you to be hijacked by emotions, but in the following assignment you will learn the steps to stop, breathe, think, and respond, rather than erupt or make unwise decisions.

Activity

1. On a piece of paper draw a straight line and number it 1 2 3 4 5. 5 is representative of being extremely stressed, 1 is little to no stress. Circle where you are right now.
2. Put everything down, spit out your gum if chewing any, sit comfortably and just listen.
3. As you do the following breathing routine imagine filling your stomach up with air, visualize and even feel a balloon being blown up, then the balloon slowly releasing air.
4. Routine:

    Take a slow, deep breath in, count slowly from one to five and breathe in that entire time.

    Exhale to the count of six, a slow exhalation through the mouth.

    Again, breathe in for the count of six, exhale through the mouth for the count of seven.

    Inhale for the count of seven, exhale through the mouth for the count of eight.

    Visualize, feel, smell the most wonderful scene in your mind, your place of peace. Keep breathing in slowly, exhaling slowly and let your mind go to the place you think of for complete relaxation. It could be the beach, the mountains, anywhere you want. Let your mind take you there. Keep inhaling and exhaling slowly. Notice the

things around you, the plants, any animals, sea life, birds, whatever you want can be in your place of peace and relaxation. Now visualize, feel, smell one little gift you are going to give yourself. For instance, if your place of peace is the beach, imagine a seashell, rock, plant, or other item. Regardless of your gift it will be one that is safe and shrinks to fit into your hand. Smell the scent of the ocean, or the scent of the forest, wherever you are notice the wonder around you. This is your magical place of peace. Allow your gift to be seen, felt, and smelled in your hand, imagine rubbing it on your cheek. Now, as it is again in your hand, I want you to notice the texture and colors of it and then slowly see it disappear into your hand, moving through your entire body bringing hope, light, and peace to you. Again, bring it to your hand, now imagine stepping back and looking at yourself with that radiant light of hope, light, and peace surrounding you. Again, let it sink into your hand. Take a slow breath in, hold it, feel the peace throughout your being, slowly exhale. Keep breathing slowly and realize that whenever you are upset you can immediately go to your safe place and imagine your gift in your hand and body bringing you greater focus, patience, and peace.
Sit quietly for a minute and allow yourself to notice the lowered tension in your body.

5. Look at that line and the stress marker you placed on it. Circle where your stress is right now.
6. Discuss this experience in class.
7. Practice this three times a day until our next class. The more you practice the faster you will be able to bring the peace to you.
8. You are inviting yourself and your higher power into this cycle of relaxation. It will strengthen your immune system and help you with everyday problems. Also note that when God is mentioned you can interpret that to fit your idea of a higher being. The important thing is to connect spiritually and soulfully within and

outside of you to help you make wiser choices and have a more peaceful quality of life.

Take time today to pause every now and then, take a deep breath of that moment, and know that God loves you. He will whisper "I love you" in a 1000 different ways.
-Mark R. Woodward

Footnote

1   Verger, R. (18 July, 2019). The apollo 11 mission as told through the astronaut's heartrate. *Popular science.*

Lesson 27

Do MY Perspectives Sabotage or Enhance MY Success?

Courtesy of PublicDomainPictures@ https://pixabay.com/
photos/winter-snow-forest-wood-holiday-19312/

The past is over and done and cannot be changed.
This is the only moment we can experience.
Deep at the center of my being there is an infinite
well of gratitude.
I now allow this gratitude to fill my heart, my body, my mind,
my consciousness, my very being.
This gratitude radiates out from me in all directions,
touching everything in my world,
and returns to me as more to be grateful for.
The more grateful I feel, the more I am aware that the
supply is endless.
-Louise Hay

Michael Dowling

The year was 1880 and there was a terrible blizzard. Michael Dowling was riding on the back of a wagon and was bounced off and landed in a snow bank. The driver could not hear his cries for help. Little Michael was left to stumble around in below zero temperatures until he finally found shelter in a haystack. When morning arrived, he realized his limbs were frozen. "Two legs, one arm and four fingers on his remaining hand and arm were amputated. Despite this Dowling went on to be a successful figure in Minnesota politics, he was a successful businessman and he "blazed the Yellowstone Trail West to Yellowstone National Park and East to Plymouth Rock," Cowley (1953)[1].

Now, the rest of the story is presented below to provide the reader an invitation to understanding the plight of the man and the courage he used to become successful in life.

Michael J. Dowling was a young man who fell from a wagon in a blizzard in Michigan when he was fourteen years of age. Before his parents discovered that he had fallen from the rear of the wagon, he had been frostbitten. His right leg was amputated almost to the hip, his left leg above the knee; his right arm was amputated; his left hand was amputated. Not much future for a young lad like that was there? Do you know what he did? He went to the board of county commissioners and he told them that if they educated him. he would pay back every penny.

During World War I, Mr. Dowling, who was at that time president of one of the largest banks in St. Paul, went to Europe to visit the soldiers—to visit those who were wounded. Upon one occasion he was in a large hotel in London, and he had before him the wounded soldiers in their wheelchairs. They were in the lobby, and he was up on the mezzanine floor. As he started to speak, he minimized the seriousness of their wounds, the fact that one had lost an eye, another had lost an arm, etc., were no grounds for complaint. And he got these fellows so wrought up that they started to boo him. Then he walked over to the stairway and down the stairs toward the lobby, telling them as he walked how fortunate they were, and they continued booing.

Finally, he sat down on one of the steps and took off his right leg. And he kept on talking and telling them how well off they were. Well, they calmed down a bit, but they still resented his remarks. Then he took off his left leg. The booing stopped and before he quit speaking, he had removed his right arm and left. There he sat, there he sat—just the stump of a body.

Michael Dowling was the president of one of the largest banks in St. Paul, Minnesota. Mr. Dowling was a great success as a man, husband, and father. He had married and was the father of five children. He finally died as the result of the strength he gave in encouraging the wounded soldiers of World War I. (Michael Dowling, a Most Inspiring Figure, 2020)[2].

Lesson

This is another example of life throwing us a curve, so to speak. This experience of having limbs frozen was certainly life-altering for Michael Dowling. He was a child when it happened. We don't have many details on his family, but we do know that somehow, he drew upon the strength within to have immense dreams and orchestrate a productive and fulfilling life for himself. He refused to give up. He refused to wallow in self-pity, or limit himself.

Activities

1. List one perception you have had in the past and have learned to change it to help you.
2. Describe how that has changed your perspective (your outlook on life).
3. Write about someone you know who has overcome many challenges.
   a. What characteristics have you learned from them?

Jan Booth, M.S.

Footnote

1   Cowley, M. (1953, May 18). Achievement. https://speeches.byu.edu/talks/matthew-cowley/achievement/

2   Michael Dowling, a Most Inspiring Figure. A Ford on a Lincoln. Found online August 10, 2020 @ https://afordonthelincoln.blogspot.com/2017/07/45-michael-dowling-most-inspiring-figure.html

Lesson 28

The "Wolf" in Disguise -
Recognizing Counterfeit Messages

We camouflage our true being before others to protect ourselves
against criticism or rejection.
This protection comes at a steep price...we are misunderstood.
When we are misunderstood, especially by family and friends
we join the 'lonely crowd.'
Worse...we tend to lose touch with our real selves.
Sidney Jourard

The "Wolf in Sheep's Clothing"

Andie was a beautiful and talented teenager. She observed others and found herself consumed with the desire to be a leader among her people. An important point to understand is that she was the *wolf in sheep's clothing.* She pretended to be concerned about the people, but the leadership she sought was one in which she would RULE, not lead, and she was smart devising a plan on how to take over the kingdom. First, she ingratiated herself with the king and his guards. She flattered them and bestowed great gifts upon those with the most authority, but what she was really doing was secretly putting them into her debt. Second, she presented very sound ideas to the head of the group, and third, she gained the king's trust. Soon, he appointed her as leader of one part of the kingdom, thinking she would be a woman of peace and integrity. Instead, she told lies, small little lies mixed with false praise, which tricked the people to follow her and turn against their king. Within a few months she had convinced her "tribe" to conquer little villages in the outlying areas until she would eventually be in control. Her first primary goal was to remove the present king and become queen of the whole kingdom.

Andie was adept at pitting one person against another and enticing them with desires for power and money. Her thirst for greed and total control was endless. She appealed to the weaknesses in mankind and promised them endless treasures and total power. Soon, her followers snuck up on the king's province and took over, eventually taking out the king. As she made her plans, she forgot the soulfulness within. Instead of seeking to help the people, which she promised, she was, instead, designing intricate strategies to rule the entire population. This occurred before modern weapons of war were made.

Andie eventually succeeded in her quest, even committing murder and other heinous crimes. As she was bragging about her greatness and demanding hard labor from her people, instead of giving them the riches she had promised, she grew in power. The people feared her. However, throughout her kingdom there were those who sought liberty, who loved others and were honest in their dealings. They were true to their families and honored the value of human life. They saw the future they were facing and quietly left during the nights to seek escape from the wicked queen. This group wanted peace and organized themselves as best as they could. She sent her gang out to kill them, but they had wisely found solace in other areas.

One day she met the leader of another civilization, not a gang but a community of people seeking to strengthen their nation, enjoy freedom, and extend peace and love to one another. Those who had left Andie's reach eventually met up with this other leader, Jourdan. His parents had taught him that he had great worth, they raised him up to lead with kindness and to work hard. "Jourdan," his mother said, "Your name means spirit warrior, and this is what you are. You are a warrior for good, for hope, for love of all people. You must remember this for there are many who will seek to deceive you. Listen to your heart and you will know if their intentions are for good or for evil."

Jourdan's mother died when he was fifteen. He mourned her death for years, but always remembered her counsel. One day his father took him aside and told him that a great war was being planned against them. He would need to be strong and courageous, a man who stood for freedom. He and his father brought their people together, sending out proclamations of love and gratitude for their loyalty and dedication to freedom, then they warned the people what was coming. They taught them in small groups how to arm themselves to withstand the battle which was being planned against them.

Andie led her gang to fight Jourdan's people. His father died in battle but Jourdan kept his focus so that he could save as many lives as possible. After several days of battle both sides were exhausted. It was then that Jourdan sent a letter to Andie asking her to meet with him, promising her that it would be a neutral zone. Initially, she refused and increased her rage against anyone going against her, engaging in even more war and killing anyone standing in her way. Jourdan realized that Andie would never agree to peace, so he provided a detailed plan to his own team of soldiers. They carried it out and were able to take Andie during the night and bring her to Jourdan. He waited anxiously for their safe return. Finally, they arrived. Andie was consumed with hatred. She spat on Jourdan and threatened him, ranting and raving over his "so-called righteousness" and telling him that power and money were the whole meaning of life. Jourdan calmly waited while she screamed. He didn't say a word, instead he just sat with hands clasped and a look of absolute peace on his face, yet sorrow in his eyes for the evil in Andie. Eventually Andie stopped her tirade and stared at him. The look would have frightened anyone else, but not Jourdan. He was so aware of the love he had for his people and for hers that it gave him added strength.

"Andie, I am so sad for you. You have chosen to deceive thousands and you have brought death to hundreds. You seek after riches and power but have no peace inside for it is never enough for you. I know the meaning of your name, do you?"

This caught her off guard. "What do you mean by the meaning of my name?" she snarled. "Well, each of us is named for one reason or another. The name "Andie" actually means a woman of courage and peace." At this she laughed, a maniacal laugh that sent chills over the soldiers, but not Jourdan. Again, she stopped and stared at him. "You will never know peace for I am the Queen and I destroy all who stand in my way."

"Andie, I am offering you peace now. A way to save lives. All I ask is that you tell your people to give up their weapons and stop fighting then we can be united as a nation, a peaceful nation." Andie leaped forward and slapped Jourdan across the face. "I will never give into your demands."

Jourdan mourned for the evil in Andie. He knew she was born with a great power to do good, to be a leader of peace but instead, she had chosen to be a leader for hatred and war. He offered her a peaceful solution again and she was seized with such rage that she grabbed the soldier's blade to kill Jourdan, but in doing so fell, the blade penetrating her own heart. Upon hearing of her death, many of her followers fled, but others turned in their weapons and became united with Jourdan in the cause for freedom.

Lesson

This is a story taken from history showing the power of good and the power of evil. It exists in our daily lives. We each have important decisions to make. Consider the choices you make every day. What to eat, what to say to someone when they "dis" you, how to treat the guards, if you are incarcerated, or your teachers, and therapists. Consider the thoughts and messages you give yourself. The question is, do you want to become a leader for peace and hope or a symbol of darkness and greed? Do you want to be someone other's trust will help them find their way and be successful in positive experiences, family, relationships, and career? This will bring you inner happiness and light. The opposite of this is greed, power, hatred, envy, and evil intent, which never brings happiness and lasting internal peace. Nor will you ever be satisfied, for as one clings to the dark side, as they talk about in Star Wars, the greed only increases, the hatred empowers, and the worth of the soul gets lost in the cloak of hopelessness. Just as Andie had planned out conquering the kingdom Jourdan had planned how to save his people, keep families safely intact, and build up a great civilization for peace.

In today's world, common tools for deception include drug abuse, pornography, bullying, cyber bullying, violence, retaliation, greed, envy, feelings of entitlement, cruelty, uncontrolled anger, manipulations, lying, and other anti-social designs. Often, they are camouflaged under the cloak that they will make things better.

Recognize deceptions for what they are. Ask yourself the following questions when you are offered a choice to do or say something.

> ➢ Will this strengthen my personal integrity?
> ➢ Will this put me in a position of addiction?
> ➢ Will this contaminate my mind?
> ➢ Will this offer momentary pleasure and lifelong conflict?
> ➢ Will this teach me to serve others with more compassion?
> ➢ Will this help me strengthen personal discipline?
> ➢ Will this help me reach my goals and move beyond them?

What did Anakin say before he allowed the hatred to consume him? "Compassion, which I would define as unconditional love, is essential to a Jedi's life. So, you might say, that we are encouraged to love." — Anakin (from Attack of the Clones). Sadly, he allowed hatred and greed to enter his heart and find residence there.

It is never too late to change, to have known the sadness and felt the rage, and now, to recognize that **your** future depends on **your** choices today. Remember, there are always people to help you, but sometimes you have to search for them. Seek out the goodness and joy, serve others, and allow your God, your higher power to have a permanent place in your heart.

Remember, A Jedi's Strength Flows From The Force.
But Beware: Anger, Fear, Aggression
– The Dark Side Are They.
Yoda to Luke in *Return of the Jedi*

Activity

1. Discuss why honesty is important.
2. Provide examples you have seen when someone has "presented" one way to you, but in truth, they were deceiving you, they were, in fact, *the wolf in sheep's clothing.*

Emotionally, spiritually, physically; emotional manipulation is a primary tool of the wolf. They like to play on heightened emotions to engage you in behaviors that benefit them. They gather people that will serve their need to be in control, whether this is through a romantic relationship, a close friendship or a strategic partnership. They make being with them fun and exciting at first, and then they shift the focus of the relationship onto them and their needs.

How to Spot a Wolf in Sheep's Clothing
https://www.powerofpositivity.com/how-to-spot-wolf-in-sheeps-clothing/

Lesson 29

The Power of Belief

Knowledge is power,
but knowledge about yourself is self-empowerment.
Joe Dispenza

Miracle Man

The man was twenty-three. He was a chiropractor, wealthy, well-liked, and lived a glamorous life. He enjoyed the competition of triathlons; running, swimming, and bike racing so he signed up for another competition. He completed the run and swimming events then hurriedly took off on his bike. An official directed him in one direction, but an SUV hit him from behind, catapulting him over his bike and onto the cement, breaking several vertebrae. Then, the vehicle kept coming and he grabbed the bumper to avoid more injuries. Finally, the car stopped, and he tumbled, completely out of control, reacting to the force of the stop, for up to twenty more yards.

This is the story of Dr. Joe Dispenza. The accident left him with six broken vertebrae in his thoracic spine (8, 9, 10, 11, 12) and lumbar 1.

This meant the injuries ran from his shoulder blades down to his kidneys. He wrote, "The vertebrae in the spine are stacked like individual blocks, and when I hit the ground with that kind of force, they collapsed and compressed from the impact. The eighth thoracic vertebra, the top segment that I broke, was more than 60 percent collapsed, and the circular arch that contained and protected the spinal cord was broken and pushed together in a pretzel-like shape. When a vertebra compresses and fractures, the bone has to go somewhere. In my case, a large volume of shattered fragments went back toward my spinal cord. It was definitely not a good picture."[1]

He suffered a variety of types of pain with numbness and tingling sensations. It was a major physical and emotional trauma. There were bone fragments on his spinal cord. The surgeons recommended that he have a Harrington rod implanted, which involved cutting out back parts of the vertebrae above and below the fractures. The rod would then be screwed and clamped on both sides of his spine, 12-inch rods. Finally, the surgeon would scrape pieces off of his hip bone and paste them over the implanted rods. With the surgery he might be able to walk again and he would also live with chronic pain.[2]

Three surgeons recommended this surgery and they needed to operate within 24-48 hours of the injury. The rod would remain in his back and provide a lifetime of limited mobility and he would no longer be able to be a chiropractor. As he lay in the hospital bed, he started to think about himself. He recognized some traits he perhaps hadn't been aware of, with such depth, before. He was smart. He knew the human body and his specialty was the back and spine. He believed in a higher power, that someone had something to do with helping each human being form and he started to believe that if he could tune into that higher power and use his knowledge to visualize and meditate on his body healing he could forego the surgery and get himself well. The doctors were furious at his decision. When the chief of surgery came by his father was visiting, looked at his son, then the chief of surgery and said, "Hey, he knows exactly what he's doing."[3]

Dr. Dispenza testified to his belief in some type of higher intelligence or what he called an invisible consciousness which has provided life for each of us, stating that "...it supports, maintains, protects, and heals us every moment. It creates almost 100 trillion specialized cells (starting from only 2), it keeps our hearts beating hundreds of thousands of times per day, and it can organize hundreds of thousands of chemical reactions in a single cell in every second—among many other incredible functions. I reasoned at the time that if this intelligence was real and if it willfully, mindfully, and lovingly had such amazing abilities, maybe I could take my attention off my external world and begin to go within and connect with it—developing a relationship with it."[4]

For the next nine and a half weeks he lay face down, everyday visualizing his back healing. 2-3 hours morning and evening focused meditation for healing. Then, he was sitting up and walking! No cast, no rod, no surgery. Less than a week later he started to see his patients again. He has since traveled the globe teaching others about the power of the mind and how important it is for each person to take an active role in their health, their view of life, their emotional and spiritual life, and to help others. He believes in all types of medical interventions and never recommends that a person quit taking medications, but he does advocate that people be part of the healing process and not just leave it up to a doctor, physical therapist or psychotherapist. Now, about 30 years post-accident, Dr. Dispenza rarely has back pain and has had a tremendous impact worldwide on helping people realize the power of belief, meditation, and communion with that higher intelligence.[5]

Dr. Joe Dispenza's personality was one which would seek solutions rather than problems. He embraced the idea of possibilities and has encouraged thousands of people to do the same. He has that internal drive to move forward with a positive, "can do" attitude, and to share hope with others. This is the challenge I put forward to each participant and trainer of this program. You are remarkable. You are here on the earth for a purpose. Why are you alive now and not 500 years ago or 100 years into the future? What is your role? What are your interests and how can you have a positive impact in your life and the life of others?

Lesson

Dr. Dispenza suffered a major injury. He was faced with difficult decisions. He alone had to decide what was best for him to do. Because of his background in medicine and his knowledge of anatomy he was able to make his decision against surgery and completely commit to inviting his body to heal. For another person the Harrington Rod operation would certainly be the wise choice. Each of us has hard decisions to make in life. The key is to understand ourselves and our capabilities. This week you are invited to take a personality inventory which will offer insights into the wonder that is YOU!

Every time we have a thought, we make a chemical.
If we have good thoughts, we make chemicals that make us feel good.
And if we have negative thoughts,
we make chemicals that make us feel exactly the way we are thinking.
-Joe Dispenza yourpositiveoasis.com/joe-dispenza-quotes
Remind yourself every single day of who you want to be
and you will cause your brain to fire in new sequences,
in new patterns, in new combinations.
And whenever you make your brain work differently,
you are changing your mind.
-Joe Dispenza yourpositiveoasis.com/joe-dispenza-quotes

Activity

1. Design a plaque on paper that represents the word belief.
2. Inside the plaque write "I Believe".
3. On the back write about a time you had to exert belief in yourself to accomplish something.
4. Add a paragraph on how you can use the power of belief to achieve something beginning right now.
5. As a class discuss the last two quotes.
6. Why are good thoughts important?
7. Why is it important to repeat positive affirmations throughout the day?

8. Discuss connecting the affirmation with emotion, which is the key to making it happen.

Footnotes

1   Dispenza, J. (23 May 2014). How I Healed Myself After Breaking 6 Vertebrae: The Placebo Effect in Action. *You Can Heal Your Life*. Retrieved (18 December 2019) from https://www.healyourlife.com/how-i-healed-myself-after-breaking-6-vertebrae

2   Harrington Rod Definition. Spine Health. https://www.spine-health.com/glossary/harrington-rod

3   Dispenza, J. & McNay, L. (n.d.) 'The Science of Changing Your Mind'. Retrieved (18 December 2019) from https://video.search.yahoo.com/search/video?fr=mcafee&p=the+science+of+change+with+joe+dispenza#id=5&vid=8ce7a0324fde9ae0f8896156cbc6e22a&action=view.

4   Dispenza, J. (23 May 2014). How I Healed Myself After Breaking 6 Vertebrae: The Placebo Effect in Action. *You Can Heal Your Life*. Retrieved (18 December 2019) from https://www.healyourlife.com/how-i-healed-myself-after-breaking-6-vertebrae.

5   Ibid.

Lesson 30

The Importance of Resiliency

You may encounter many defeats,
but you must not be defeated.
In fact, it may be necessary to encounter the defeats,
so you can know who you are,
what you can rise from,
how you can still come out of it.
— **Maya Angelou**

There are times in life so filled with strife and sorrow that we need pause and secure that inner resiliency so desperately needed to face all there is in life. By tuning into your heart and faith you open the doorway to healing and courage. Though it may be difficult to remain optimistic it is imperative to recognize the blessings you have. By focusing on the negative, you will feel your energy sagging and your emotions being ignited into despondency, hopelessness, and despair. An important component of resiliency is recognizing those little messages our bodies and minds, our hearts and souls send us. Be aware of your thoughts and learn to switch to a mindset of optimism and hope. Make a collage or drawing of dreams. List all that you are grateful for.

<u>Inmates and Gratitude</u>: In asking inmates in a prison to keep a gratitude list I found their comments inspiring: toothpaste, sheets, food, not being on lockdown, having someone smile at them, sharing a book or idea with someone…the list went on and on. These were men and women incarcerated in a prison. And the most common item listed was that they had been caught and put in prison because it forced them to change. Finally, they realized that they could continue the path they were on or take the opportunities offered by prison programs and therapeutic interventions to get them the help they needed.

Lesson

There are lessons to be learned in life. When we choose to step back and analyze our situations and experiences, we are inviting greater personal awareness. With this, we can then determine what we can do better in the future to ensure our physical and emotional health, honor the spirituality at our core, and determine what course of action to take to empower us on our journey.

Activities:

Consider the following checklist on the cons and pros of resiliency. Look at this through two lenses, your own life, and that of someone you are concerned about. Keep the list handy for the discussion post. There is a great cost when we simply take the negative outlet. The cost is to our integrity, the fall-out to self, family, and community. I ask you to consider each statement honestly for yourself and for that other person, then think about what you do that is healthy and resilient and what they do that you admire.

Cost-Benefit Resiliency Chart

COST	BENEFIT
Dang, I have to take responsibility for my actions.	I am capable and willing to take responsibility for my actions.
Blame & Project	Accept & own the problem
Rationalize and/or Deny	Admit
Play the Victim	Be the courageous achiever
Hopelessness	Nurture faith and hope
Self-Anesthetize	Seek help
Give up	Conquer, continue taking one step forward
If I create chaos, I feel that I am in control	I am a peacemaker
If I triangulate relationships, I feel that I am in control	I choose to build bridges
I crave the approval of others	I am at peace with myself
Other's opinion of me determines my actions	For the most part I make my own decisions and honor those
If I complain enough, I get what I want	I make honorable choices to pursue those things most important to me
I depend upon others to fill my needs	I draw on the resources within to fill my needs
I experience a lot of anxiety	I rarely feel anxious
I feel overwhelmed with my anxiety	I have developed tools to deal with the anxiety issues I have
I experience depression	I rarely feel depressed
I experience overwhelming depression	I have resources I access to get help during depressive episodes
I feel like giving up	When I feel like giving up, I resolve to keep trying, and if I need help, I ask for it
I have no power to make my life better	I have the internal motivation to make my life better and understand that sometimes I will need help

Lesson 31

Living and Being a Person of Peace

Carefully watch your thoughts, for they become your words.
Manage and watch your words, for they will become your actions.
Consider and judge your actions;
for they have become your habits.
Acknowledge and watch your habits,
for they shall become your values.
Understand and embrace your values,
for they become your destiny.
— **Mahatma Gandhi**

A Man of Peace - Mahatma Gandhi

Mohandas K. Gandhi was born in Porbandar, India in October 2, 1869 – January 30, 1948. He became known as Mahatma, which translates as "…a person to be revered for high-mindedness, wisdom, and selflessness…a person of great prestige in a field of endeavor." https://www.merriam-webster.com/dictionary/mahatma.

Other names for Mahatma were Bapu, meaning father (webster.com) and later referred to as a father for the nation because he was so beloved.

When Mahatma, was only 13 years old, he married 14-year-old Kasturbai Makhanji in an arranged marriage, which was the custom at that time in history. (Mohandes Gandhi...World History Project, 2020) [1]. They also reported that young Gandhi was a very spiritually minded man and studied many of the world's religious writings, "The religious spirit within me became a living force." He became immersed in Hindu spirituality and writings, then committed himself to a life of humility and fasting. His mother was a humble woman, and one devoted to spirituality and religion. She had a major influence on Gandhi. Her religious devotion provided strength to her throughout life and had a profound impact on Gandhi. He translated the Hindu text Bhagavad Gita, which led him to a study of Indian scriptures and he also studied the Bible. He was very touched by the teachings of Jesus Christ and loved the scriptures and messages on humility and forgiveness, which he readily adopted into his own life, Mahatma Gandhi Biography (2018) [2].

Gandhi's law education gave him knowledge and experience but as he practiced law in South Africa he was alarmed at the intensity of racial discrimination and injustices against the Indian population. He began his non-violent protests, calling them satyagraha, which was "...a policy of political resistance, especially that advocated by Mahatma gandhi against British rule in India. (Found online @ https:///www.bing.com/search?FORM=U527DF&PC=U5ˢᵗ&q=define+satyagraha).

Gandhi's work resulted in imprisonment on several occasions. He campaigned against heavy British rule but also supported them in some areas, even being decorated for his work during the Boer War and Zulu rebellion.

In 1915, Gandhi returned to India after having spent 21 years in South Africa. In 1915 where he was elected leader of the Indian nationalist movement and successfully organized a series of non-violent protests, including one to two-day strikes. He encouraged his fellow Indians to incorporate inner discipline in their daily lives. He believed they needed to prove they were ready for independence, was it right for India to self-govern? He wanted to strengthen the people first with peaceful ideals and self-restraint. Some other Indian factions were more militant, seeking to overthrow the British. Gandhi went about it with the attitude of peace and love. In fact, if he heard of violence or rioting, he would call off planned protests.

In 1930 he led the famous Salt March in protest to the Salt Acts which took money from the Indians by importing salt from other countries. Hundreds were arrested, but he stayed true to his cause. When the more militant faction killed some British civilians, Gandhi terminated the independence movement because he did not believe India was ready yet to stand on their own. This encouraged some of the more radical Indians.

Following WWII Britain gave India their independence but planned to divide India into two countries: India and Pakistan. Gandhi opposed the idea believing that Muslims and Hindus could co-exist peacefully, even including Hindu, Muslim, and Christian prayers at his meetings. His work failed. The separation occurred, and, despite his prayers, fasts, and appeals sectarian violence and killings followed the partition.

Gandhi was adamant against the Hindu Caste system. There was one caste labeled "untouchable" and Gandhi ministered to them, many having leprosy. He worked diligently to stop prejudices that had been reinforced for centuries.

When he was 78 years old, he underwent a long fast to prevent sectarian killing, then after five days of fasting the leaders stopped the killings. Ten days later Gandhi was assassinated by a Hindu Brahmin, a man who opposed Gandhi's support for the untouchables and Muslims, reported (Pettinger, 2011)[3]. Gandhi was a person of peace, he loved his people and sought to teach them the doctrines of peace, and he lived with a strong basis of faith and perseverance. To the end of his life, he dedicated himself to his people and held onto hope in spite of strife and reactionary violence.

When every hope is gone, 'when helpers fail and comforts flee,'
I find that help arrives somehow, from I know not where.
Supplication, worship, prayer are no superstition;
they are acts more real than the acts of

eating, drinking, sitting or walking.
It is no exaggeration to say that they alone are real, all else is unreal.

– Gandhi Autobiography – *The Story of My Experiments with Truth*[4]

Footnotes

1   Mohandes gandhi marries kasturbai makhanji in an arranged child marriage. (2020). World history project. The history of us. Retrieved from https://worldhistoryproject.org/1883/5/mohandes-gandhi-marries-kasturbai-makhanji-in-an-arranged-child-marriage

2   Mahatma gandhi biography. (1 March, 2018). *Biography Online.* Retrieved from https://www.biographyonline.net/politicians/indian/gandhi.html

3   Pettinger, T. (2011). "Biography of Mahatma Gandhi. Oxford, UK. *www.biographyonline.net* 12th Jan 2011. Last updated 1 March 2018.

4   Ibid.

Lesson 32

Making a Difference: The Power of One

Human progress is neither automatic nor inevitable...
Every step toward the goal of justice requires
sacrifice, suffering, and struggle;
the tireless exertions and passionate concern
of dedicated individuals.
Martin Luther King

Martin Luther King, Jr. January 15, 1929 – April 4, 1968

January 15, 1929 was the day an infant was born who would, in his lifetime, be known worldwide for his work on civil rights. Martin Luther King, Jr. grew up to be a Baptist Minister. He achieved a lot in his thirty-nine years of life. He directed the Southern Christian Leadership Conference (SCLC), prompted the Civil Rights Act of 1964 as well as the Voting Rights Act of 1965. In 1964 he was awarded the Nobel Peace Prize and was one of the most well-known and influential African American leaders in history, Martin Luther King (2020)[1].

A glimpse of his history shows his father as a strong civil rights activist, also, believing that slavery and cruelty were against God's laws. Martin

161

Luther King's father and grandfather were ministers and strived diligently to make a difference.

Dr. King started school at 5. He skipped the 9th and 11th grades and, at the young age of 15, began his college studies at the Morehouse College in Atlanta in 1944. Initially, he decided not to go into the Ministry. Things changed, though, when was a junior in college. He took one Bible class, which renewed his faith and background in theology and made the choice to become a minister. In 1948 he earned his bachelor's degree from Morehouse College, then went onto Chester, Pennsylvania's Crozer Theological Seminary where he excelled. Not only was he elected student body president, he was also the class valedictorian. The year was 1951.

Dr. King's pathway was riddled with controversy and problems. He drank a lot of beer, frequented pool halls and fell in love with a Caucasian woman, all blatant acts against the conservative beliefs his father and mother raised him with. Then, during his senior year, the preside of Morehouse College, Benjamin E. Mays, mentored him. Mays was adamant and outspoken about civil rights, racial equality and taught Dr. King to view Christianity as the means to awaken the nation and bring forth social change. Dr. King went onto enroll in a doctoral program at Boston University, where he met and fell in love with Coretta Scott. She was a singer and musician attending Boston's New England Conservator school. They married in June of 1953 later having four children. The next year, 1954, he was made pastor of the Dexter Avenue Baptist Church in Montgomery, Alabama. He completed his dissertation and graduated with his Ph. D. in 1955 at the age of 25.

Changes began happening on March 2, 1955. A fifteen-year-old girl, Claudette Colvin, refused to stand up and give her seat to a white man. For that simple statement of freedom, she was taken to jail! On December 1, 1955, a tired, hard-working 42-year-old Rosa Parks got on a bus to go home after work and sat on the front row of the designated "colored" section. Several white men didn't have a place to sit so the bus driver ordered the "black" people to give up their seats, three complied, Rosa Parks refused. She was arrested for supposedly breaking the Montgomery city code and was fined ten dollars, then an additional four dollars for court fees, which were huge sums of money to Rosa.

The arrest of Rosa Parks became a pivotal point in King's life. The head of the local NAACP (National Association for the Advancement of Colored People) chapter, E. D. Nixon organized a meeting with King and other leaders to plan the "Montgomery bus boycott." The group elected King to lead the boycott, he was young, had strong family connections, and was a professional. He was new to their area, they viewed him as having a credible influence. In his first speech as their president he stated, "We have no alternative but to protest. For many years we have shown an amazing patience. We have sometimes given our white brothers the feeling that we liked the way we were being treated. But we come here tonight to be saved from that patience that makes us patient with anything less than freedom and justice." (Martin Luther King, 2020)[2].

This was a primary factor in King's leadership, as well as promoting the cause of freedom forward, and had a serious impact on the bus industry. For 382 days, the African American people of that area walked to work. They suffered harassment, intimidation, and acts of violence. King's and Nixon's homes were focal points for attacks. As a result, the African American community took legal action. They claimed the city ordinance was unconstitutional because it was founded on the Supreme Court's decision that "separate is never equal" coming out of the Brown v. Board of Education case. It was an uphill, costly battle, but eventually Montgomery city finally revoked the law that mandated segregated public transportation. This prompted the African American civil rights leaders to establish a supportive national organization. King, Ralph Abernathy, and 60 civil rights activists and leaders initiated the Southern Christian Leadership Conference, creating a coordinated effort with community and churches to conduct non-violent reform and promote civil rights. From there they started the right to vote process by registering black voters.

Dr. King found inspiration in Mahatma Gandhi's non-violent activism approach and visited his place of birth in India. This had a profound effect on him, and he devoted his life to American civil rights and non-violent protests. By 1960 he was getting more national exposure. On October 19,

1960, he and 75 students went into a department store for lunch. They sat at the counter but were refused service, then arrested, but charges were soon dropped so the city's reputation would not be affected. Then, he was again arrested for an unpaid traffic ticket. President Kennedy heard of the incident and contacted King's wife. His role got politics involved, which meant pressure on the city and again, he was released.

1963 brought increased changes when King organized a non-violent protest in Birmingham, Alabama. Families were involved in a peaceful meeting and the city police turned fire hoses and dogs on the demonstrators. He and many others were arrested, and King was admonished for endangering the lives of children, but he did not back down.

The historic march on Washington took place on August 28, 1963. More than 200,000 people were there, in front of the Lincoln Memorial and this is the place for his "I Have a Dream" speech. "I have a dream that my four children will one day live in a nation where they will not be judged by the color of their skin but by the content of their character." This event propelled the Civil Rights Act of 1964 which authorized the federal government to make sure all schools and public owned facilities were desegregated. This is the year he earned the Nobel Peace Prize.

Sadly, King faced a lot of opposition. Violence erupted on March 7, 1965 during a civil rights march from Selma to Montgomery, Alabama. He was not there but saw it on television and a planned second march was canceled. A third march was planned, which King attended. 2500 marchers gathered on March 9, 1965 to cross the Pettus Bridge but when they encountered state troopers, they humbly knelt in prayer, then turned back, led by King. Then, on March 21, 1965 about 2,000 people, black and white, gathered to march from Selma to Montgomery ending with approximately 25,000 marchers! The event was televised. Five months later the 1965 Voting Rights Act was signed by President Johnson. Dr. King kept marching and interestingly, he appealed to the white population, but some militant blacks opposed him. Understandably, Dr. King was getting tired. The increased criticism, backlash, public challenges, living under threat and repeatedly going to jail were wearing him down. On April 3, 1968 he gave his final speech, "I've Been to the Mountaintop" and told the

Mason Temple supporters of Memphis, Tennessee, "I've seen the promised land. I may not get there with you. But I want you to know tonight that we, as a people, will get to the promised land." Martin Luther King (2020)[3].

Martin Luther King was killed the next day, while standing on a balcony adjacent to his room at the Lorraine Motel. The sniper, James Earl Jones, was arrested two months later. This created a violent backlash across the nation with demonstrations and riots in more than 100 cities. Jones pled guilty in 1969 and died in prison on April 23, 1998.

Martin Luther King was a complicated man. He worked hard for civil rights and encouraged peaceful protests. His record is one showing a man with flaws and a man with courage.

Lesson

The lesson is about releasing the past. It is an invitation to you to understand and act upon your own power to build a better future for yourself. Martin Luther King wanted freedom for himself, his family, and his nation of people. Each of us carries emotional baggage. To ensure a brighter future it is important to be able to compartmentalize different areas of life. To do so requires, intelligence, creativity, and empowering self with new habits.

Activity

1. Draw a trunk or case.
2. Inside the trunk or case put sentences of words of past wounds.
3. Put a lock on it.
4. Visualize this, take a breath in and release negative feelings. See, hear, feel them go into the trunk to be locked up.
5. When you are ready, imagine those issues flying away.
6. Draw another trunk. Inside this write the positive values you want to lock in your heart and keep with you each day, to bring hope and peace to others.

Jan Booth, M.S.

Footnote

1   Martin Luther King. (2020, January 14). *Biography*. https://www.biography.com/activist/martin-luther-king-jr

2   Ibid.

3   Ibid.

Lesson 33

Addiction: A Thorn in the Soul

Our greatest glory is not in never failing,
but in rising up every time we fail.
— Ralph Waldo Emerson

A Giant Step Towards Sobriety

In 1935 Bill Wilson, who was later known as Bill W. joined with Dr. Robert Smith, or Dr. Bob, to begin a program to help alcoholics. It became known as Alcoholics Anonymous. History of Alcoholics Anonymous)[1]. This organization has helped millions. It was started by an alcoholic, a person who knew the extreme power it had over his life.

How does one cut the chains that bind them to the past? Addiction is a hole, a vacuum that pulls a person in and drains the will to succeed out of them. But there is help available and there are millions of people who have walked the pathway of addiction of one form or another who are willing to help. There is always a hand to pull the person out of the abyss if they choose to reach for it. That is the critical factor; is the person ready to make the choice to give up the addiction? Each of our problems can be faced if we simply start to say, "I can do this." Then, follow that with one step towards positive action, let faith in yourself and your higher power work, seek help, be humble, and grasp the hand of the one offering this new, addiction-free way of life.

> *Everything can be taken from a man but one thing: the last of human freedoms - to choose one's attitude in any given set of circumstances, to choose one's own way.*
> *Viktor E. Frankl*

Lesson

Consider the following picture. Addiction is the process of taking one step into a hole that can pull you in so completely that it is difficult to see your way out. And, the addict keeps returning to the hole, sinking in more fully each time. It enters the mind and wraps its' tentacles around the soul to claim victory over agency. But, there is still the opportunity to declare triumph over self, to become the altruistic, honest, and compassionate being you were born to be. Instead of walking to the hole, you walk in the opposite direction. Often, this requires new friends, medical intervention, counseling, and change in lifestyle. But what is the common denominator? It is you, claiming your right to freedom of choice, and you digging within to find the courage and determination to do what it takes to free yourself from the chains that bind you.

This lesson began with the story of Bill W. and the introduction of the 12-Step Program for alcoholism. However, the lesson is directed towards anyone with any addiction and their power to leave it behind if they so choose. One person reported his own struggle, "I knew one drink could pull me under, take me to that inner darkness that is nearly impossible to conquer. I remembered my promise to God and myself. I reached for the hands of loved ones who cared, and I honored the commitment to leave the past behind." (anonymous source)

You have a power in you that is greater than any thorn in your life. It is up to you. Isn't that powerful information? Embracing your own inner power and leaning on a higher source for added strength are key factors for releasing those entanglements that have controlled your life. Recognizing trigger points, understanding your own pain and conflicts invites introspection and wisdom. The first step is to admit you are powerless over _____. I leave that blank so you can fill it in. Now, look at step two: a power greater than self will provide you with the added support to overcome your challenge. You have the power to remove the barbs of addiction and embrace the freedom that will follow. And, the third step locks in the healing process, you make the decision, it is your choice to turn your life over to your higher power, your God. He is there for you each step of the way. It is one thing to believe in a higher power, it is another to learn to turn to that lasting source of love and invite Him into your life. Just as a cactus has barbs that stick, addiction has mental controls that attach and feed on themselves. You have the power to remove the barbs and find your freedom.

Learn to recognize those inner conflicts that nag at your soul.
They are the thorns in your life,
The piercing sting of unresolved grief,
leading to irresponsible anger and self-sabotaging behaviors.
They are there to teach you.
Go to their source and release their toxins.
Jan C. Booth

Activities

1. Review the 12 Steps of AA and highlight those where you see a potential problem for yourself. Remember, addiction can include alcohol, other drugs, gambling, pornography, procrastination, stealing, cheating, rage cycles, even a negative attitude.
2. Discuss which steps you feel are most important for you.

AA 12 Steps

1. We admitted we were powerless over alcohol – that our lives had become unmanageable.

2. We came to believe that a power greater than ourselves could restore us to sanity.

3. We made a decision to turn our will and our lives over to the care of God as we understood Him.

4. Made a searching and fearless moral inventory of ourselves.

5. Admitted to God, to ourselves, and to another human being the exact nature of our wrongs.

6. Were entirely ready to have God remove all these defects of character.

7. Humbly asked Him to remove our shortcomings.

8. Made a list of all persons we had harmed and became willing to make amends to them all.

9. Made direct amends to such people wherever possible, except when to do so would injure them or others.

10. Continued to take personal inventory and when we were wrong promptly admitted it.

11. Sought through prayer and meditation to improve our conscious contact with God, as we understood Him, praying only for knowledge of His will for us and the power to carry that out.

12. Having had a spiritual awakening as the result of these Steps, we tried to carry this message to alcoholics, and to practice these principles in all our affairs.

https://www.recovery.org/alcoholics-anonymous/ January 17, 2020

Footnote

1   Alcoholics Anonymous. History of Alcoholics Anonymous). (en.wikipedia. org/wiki/History_of_Alcoholics_Anonymous).

Lesson 34

Letting Go – The Road to Healing

> *To forgive is to set a prisoner free*
> *and discover that the prisoner was you.*
> **-Lewis B. Smedes**

Rambo an Extremely Angry Ram

Kathleen Stevens and her team ran an animal sanctuary. One day a ram they very cleverly named Rambo, arrived. He had suffered terrible abuse and neglect and had been confined for years. He was angry! She wrote that he was filled with anger and testosterone. His ewes, fourteen in number, cowered in the corner and Rambo would charge everyone him, Stevens (2009, kindle dx version).[1]

He smashed fences, tore down doors, and attacked anyone who happened to get in his way. He had everything he needed, never lacking in love, food, and shelter. Sadly, nothing seemed to calm the ram, so the team nicknamed him Rambo. He was cantankerous and mean, knocked down fences, plowed through doors and endlessly caused bruises and pain among the caretakers. Even neutering didn't help. For two years they worked with him, then wondered if it was time to sell him to another sanctuary. Do we ever get to a point of giving up on someone or even ourselves? Well, at that point "Carol" came on board, a wise and caring woman who seemed to sense each animal's needs. She told Kathleen that Rambo just needed more time, certainly not to give up on him. Slowly, over the next few months his outbursts lessened, and he began to bond with the team. The author writes:

> Was it something else altogether? Our prisons are filled with people whose bleak circumstances lead them to violence. It is the rare individual who frees himself from his past and lives the remainder of his life with purpose and compassion. People like these are rare individuals, Rambo was finally able to leave his past—prolonged starvation and years of imprisonment in a filthy stall crammed with animals – behind. It had taken nearly two long years, but Rambo was no longer a threat. Still, who he would become we could not have fathomed…not in our wildest dreams. (Stevens, 2009, kindle dx version 19%)[1].

Rambo released his anger, bonded with Kathy's dog, and even began being a type of "nanny" to other animals. One evening he warned Kathy that the two turkeys she lovingly carried outside in the daytime and brought in at night, had been left out in the rain and cold. How did he communicate this? As usual, on that night Kathleen went into the barn to check all her animals and say goodnight to them (horses, pigs, ducks, chickens, roosters, goats, sheep, and cows). Suddenly Rambo charged her, then stopped directly in front and bleated. She sensed something was wrong and asked him to somehow show her what was wrong. Rambo then marched down the aisle and made an abrupt turn to show Kathy the empty turkey stall. She ran outside and rescued the two birds, dried and fed them, all the while apologizing as Rambo looked on. She wrote:

> It was time to thank Rambo. In the darkened, hushed barn aisle, I sat on my knees and looked into his eyes. "Thank you, Rambo. Thank you for telling me about the turkeys. What a good job you did…what a good, good job." I took his face in my hands and massaged his woolly cheeks." (Stevens, 2009, kindle dx version 21%)[2].

When you let something go,
Something magical happens.
You give God room to work.
-Lifehack

Lesson

Rambo arrived at the sanctuary filled with fear. His healing came through the persistent effort of kindness, just as we need that in our daily lives. Sometimes we do not recognize the help others offer, but if we humble ourselves and take a small step into trust, we can open the doorway for healing. The following activities involve your ability to empower yourself to let go of the past and move into the present and future with clarity and hope.

Activity

1. Draw a bridge.
2. On one side of the bridge use colors to depict your past. Some will be bright and cheerful, others darker.
3. Design the bridge with symbols of hope.
4. Use colors to highlight the bridge, to make it uplifting and interesting.
5. On the other side of the bridge sketch a scene that depicts your future, one filled with joy success, and the awareness of your own worth.

> *When you let something go,*
> *Something magical happens.*
> *You give God room to work.*
> Author Unknown

Footnote

1 Stevens, Kathy. (2009). *Where the Blind Horse Sings: Love and Healing At An Animal Sanctuary.* NY: Skyhorse Publishing.
2 Ibid.

Lesson 35

Enthusiasm - Live Your Dream!

When you're a winner you're always happy,
But if you're happy as a loser you'll always be a loser.
-Mark Fidrych

Detroit Tigers "Bird"

The city of Detroit Michigan was in trouble. People from all types of job were laid off and the city was crumbling. It was the end of the Vietnam period and the crisis of Watergate. Detroit was in the throes of an economic recession. Gang violence and other crimes were taking over the city. It was a city severely oppressed. Even the Detroit Tigers baseball team was in a slump. In the years from 1974-75, they were losing, and their fans were falling away. Then, along came a gangly, tall, thin, young man, Mark Fidyrich, a fireball of excitement, joy, and hope. The "Bird" fever took over and 20,000 people went to see him play. He would move and dance, talk to the ball, even clean the home plate. He was a new type of athlete. His exuberance was relentless. Rusty Staub, a fellow player, said,

"He was like a shooting star." This is the story of Mark Fidyrich, taken from the MLB Network (2016)[1].

It was the 10th round of the 1974 draft when he was made the Tiger's pitcher. He was passionate about baseball and the teammates. Dave Roberts, the pitcher for the Tigers got the flu so Mark was put into the game. His first game brought life to the team and the city of Detroit. He was fun to watch, as stated, he even talked to the ball and openly congratulated other players, and by the sixth inning, had pitched a no-hitter. The Tigers won the game 2-1. The next game they lost, then the next six they won. The games were not yet televised so his notoriety came through the radio or in articles.

He was later nicknamed the Bird because someone watched him pitch, play, walk, and jump with enthusiasm and he reminded him of Big Bird on Sesame Street. The nickname stuck. As they drew near the end of the season and were facing the Yankees in the playoffs for the Pennant in 1976 and Billy Martin, the Yankees coach asked Bob Uecker about "the Bird," stating that "…If he beats us, I'll eat my hat at home plate," (Comment to Bob Uecker). No, Mr. Martin did not eat his hat when they lost, but he was certainly impressed with the Bird. That game was televised, and he kept everyone captivated with his antics and extreme pitching ability. The fans cheered, "Let's go Mark!" "Let's go Mark!" 50,000 people were in attendance! At the beginning of the 9th inning the Tigers had the lead. They won! This was the Pennant, and they were headed to the World Series. No one left. They waited to see him, so his coach ordered him to go back out and greet the people. He was amazed they wanted to see him and were willing to wait. Dan Epstein, a writer and Michigan native stated, "It was this seismic wave of emotion."

His fame dominated. The Tiger's record was 9 and 2 at mid-season, and he was named the American League's starting pitcher. Two weeks after the game he met Elton John backstage at one of his concerts. President Ford met him, and Frank Sinatra invited him to a party and spent the evening just talking with Mark. He was endorsed by the Aqua Velva after shave company and did television commercials. And, most importantly, attendance nearly tripled when he played in Detroit. People gave him money to raise his salary, people who were poor would donate a dollar because he brought such joy to them and their city and they wanted to raise his meager salary. His season ended with 19 wins and 9 loss record.

In 1977 the people were excited to see him, he was on the cover of multiple magazines, not just sports, but Rolling Stone, as well, the only baseball player to have that notoriety. He was a type of counter-culture hero.

That same year, Mark arrived at spring training. As usual, he was filled with energy and doing funny things, but the coach disciplined him to calm down because he did not want him to get hurt. He ignored the advice, fell, tore the cartilage in his right knee and had surgery. Two months post-surgery he returned to play and pitched five great games. After eight games, he suffered intense pain, and his arm went dead, he simply could not pitch. He had tendonitis in his right shoulder, so he was ordered to rest and do rehabilitation. He could not return to baseball until the next year. He still was not ready but played and hurt his shoulder again. In 1979 he tried to pitch but the tendonitis was grueling, and the doctors were not sure how to treat him to get him better. At that time, there was not a lot of knowledge on how to help with shoulder injuries. He struggled with depression, fell back to the minor leagues. At the end of the 1980s season, he returned to the major league, but his arm was too damaged for him to play. He was released from The Detroit Tigers. By 1983 he had to completely give up baseball. He stated that he wished it would have lasted longer, but that he had loved the time he had playing. Later, they realized he had been dealing with a torn rotator cuff.

Mark left baseball and immediately resumed a more normal lifestyle, buying a farm and truck, working in Chet's Diner, and doing other odd jobs. One day he went into Chet's Diner, and met his future bride. "My happy today is my daughter, my wife, and my farm." He had one child and drove a truck he named Jessica, in her name.

His fans had not forgotten him and when he returned to Detroit, they would have him suit up and greet the people. This was a shock to his daughter, who was too young to understand the powerful influence he had on people.

On April 13, 2009, Chet's opened at 5:30 AM. His sister went in and Mark waited on her. He returned to his farm and had to repair his truck. His daughter stated that she felt something was wrong, and she was correct. He had been under his truck, working on the drive shaft and his shirt had gotten entangled in it. No one was around. He suffocated and was found hours later. Mark was only 54 years old. People across the U. S. grieved his death.

Mark Fidrych exemplified humility, gratitude, and an immense love for life. He taught people not to complain, but to strive to be their best and to make life meaningful. His daughter was surprised at the great impact he had on others. The viewing and time spent honoring him lasted more than seven hours. Two months after his death Detroit Tigers invited his wife and daughter to the first game of the season and his daughter threw the first pitch.

Mark had no regrets, remained humble, with his eyes firmly set on his priorities, his wife and daughter. Mark Fidrych was a man who had enthusiasm and passion for baseball, for his work following his major league career, and most of all for his family. As a tribute to him the family started The Mark Fidrych Foundation to help handicapped children.

The Bird swooped down out of nowhere in 1976, stole the game of baseball away from the mercenaries, who considered it merely business, and gave it back to the fans.
— Doug Wilson, The Bird: The Life and Legacy of Mark Fidrych

Lesson:

Mark Fidrych was born with talent, but he also worked hard to develop that love of pitching into a profound skill. His enthusiasm for the sport did not stop there but moved into all aspects of his life and in spite of the accolades of praise he always remained the hometown boy, humble, and fun-loving, kind, considerate, and generous.

Activity:

1. Imagine being a super-hero and list your powers.
2. Define how you will help society.
3. Sketch a symbol for yourself.
4. Describe how you can be a super-hero of sorts in your life right now and define where you can make a positive difference.

Footnote

1   MLB Network (Producers) (2016, July 10). The bird. *MLB Network.*

Lesson 36

The Healing Power of Love and Faith

We don't forget the past, the wounds sometimes run deep, but we can grab hold of today and each tomorrow with renewed faith that we can be the one to bring hope and light to others.
— **Jan C. Booth**

The Healing Power of Love and Faith

The young man had a deep understanding of life. As a boy of five he had lost his father to cancer. When he was 25 his mother contracted cancer and died a few months later. As he went through this journey of being the man of the home, and helping siblings, a wife, and children, he felt the grief at a very heavy level. But there was something different about him, Robert was strong. He was filled with a knowledge of life beyond his years. At the age of five he had assumed the role of being "the man" trying to take care of his mother and sister in his innocent way, as only a little boy could interpret. His mother was a symbol of strength and determination and lived with a commonsense approach to life and frequent, joyous outbursts of laughter. Her great love and guidance offered Robert and his little sister

181

a solid foundation. She was also connected with her mother and siblings, other important sources of support for each of them.

As Robert grew, he had to consider things. He had always been responsible, but, as with teenagers a part of him wanted to rebel. He did not want to move when he was twelve, he didn't want to have to live far away from friends, and he was angry. But, little by little he accepted his situation, a new father, and with that, a new lifestyle. He lovingly welcomed two little brothers into his heart and guided them through the years. At one point in his questioning of the trials of life he realized he had to release the past. He could not get his father back. He couldn't move back to where his friends were. He threw himself into sports and having fun as a teenager, but beneath the surface was a young man missing the companionship of a little 12-year-old girl in his old neighborhood.

Robert had to adjust so he made immediate and long-term goals. Through the years he and the young woman kept in touch, and, as they entered college they still talked and made plans to one day see each other. There were occasional visits through the years. The boy brought great depth and fun to the girl's life and she brought joy and laughter to his heart. Finally, after ten years of separation the two met up and found their love for one another had simply grown and flourished through the years of separation. They married and lived happily for several years. Then, one day he got the devastating news that his mother had cancer. Again, he had to "man" up and remain strong for his immediate family, siblings, and stepfather. Again, he realized that by holding onto anger and regret he would become bitter and self-centered. How could he handle this physically, emotionally, intellectually, and spiritually? Again, he searched within, reaching into his sources of faith, there he found that solid foundation of strength, hope, and courage. The seeds of love and worth had been planted during gestation and in his early years by a devoted mother and father, and these seeds had been nurtured to bring inner security and faith in the life of the man while his mother was alive, through a second marriage and the love of his own and extended family.

When our emotional health is in a bad
state, so is our level of self-esteem.

We have to slow down and deal with what is troubling us,
so that we can enjoy the simple joy
of being happy and at peace with ourselves.
-Jess C. Scott

Lesson:

How does one embrace life yet shield oneself from grief that controls them? It is important to recognize and feel one's sorrow, and part of that is learning to compartmentalize and be able to visit the grief periodically, and to rejoice in the memories of the loved ones so greatly missed. Grief is a tender issue. You can build a brick wall to hide the pain, then a chunk of it falls out and the grief spills over. You acknowledge it, feel it, then put it away and continue on with life knowing that at some future point you might need to once again walk in the circle of pain but realizing that each time you do you come away with greater pearls of wisdom.

Activity:

1. Write an essay about a tender grief in your own life.
2. Describe the people who helped you through it.
3. What did you learn from it about yourself?

Lesson 37

The Heart of Happiness: I AM of Worth

"One human life is worth more than all the treasures of the earth."
— **Seth Adam Smith, <u>Rip Van Winkle and the Pumpkin Lantern</u>**

Two Amazing Elephants

The setting was Burman, India, around 1929. James Howard Williams was in Burma building bridges. One day as he was working, he observed an elephant attempting to carry a bundle of logs that were cradled in his tusk and trunk, but as the bull began the ascent up a steep grade he could sense the logs slipping. The elephant struggled, then calmly laid the logs down and picked up a bamboo stake. Williams stated that the elephant positioned the bamboo in his mouth, pointed it into the position of a backstop, then grasped the logs again, now securing them with the stake. Williams was amazed at the intelligence of this and other elephants. This is an interesting story presented by Victoria Croke in 2015.[1]

Early June one year, the monsoons picked up. James Williams waited for the torrential rains to loosen a huge stockpile of 2,000 teak logs. These logs had been lined up on a dried river bed. They ran smallest to largest. The last log lay 40 feet in the rear of the pile. The bundle was stuck until the rains hit. Williams had another problem. This pile of logs was eight miles upstream. The new railway bridge was secured eight miles downstream. When the rains came, they would release the logs too quickly, which would result in them taking out the support beams (piers) of the bridge. Williams immediately asked for two specific elephants, Poo Ban and Poo Gyi. These were two tuskers known for great weight and strength, and also recognized as "wise old animals- *lane bah these*," (Croke, 2015)[2].

Williams had the idea to train the two elephants to stand in the stream and when the logs came, they would re-direct them away from the sides, into the midstream to travel under the bridge. Each elephant had a rider who loved and cared for them. They immediately directed the elephants to the river and shouted, "coming left, coming right." Immediately the elephants responded in directed fashion and grasped each log that came to them and lifted it, then placed it where directed. Finally, the rains came, and the stream soon turned into a heavy river, the color of the water becoming more and more dirty with debris and silt. Crowds gathered to watch, everyone nervous except the elephants who faced their challenge with strength and focus. "They strolled out slowly dignified and magnificent – two beautiful gray tuskers wading in a brown river. The water splashed up as they moved, first darkening their legs, then skimming their bellies," Williams reported. The riders rode with confidence in their animals as they placed them in the river, then they dismounted and scurried to the hillside to observe.

The two bull elephants were accurately redirecting the logs to the center of the river to flow under the bridge. "Left tusk, right tusk" were their directives. As each piece of wood came near the bridge one of the elephants would expertly toss to the center of the current, away from the piers. Soon, the animals did another amazing thing...they positioned themselves to be able to extend their trunks frontward to slow the force.

They had incredible strength and fortitude, but after several hours they seemed to grow weary. Williams and the trainers were concerned about this. The heat was fierce and the work overwhelming. Yet, as they grew more tired they turned, in what seemed like synchronized unity, and faced downstream. The riders yelled at them thinking the elephants were quitting, but the elephants weren't! They then assumed an unusual posture, plunging their forefeet into the sandy bottom of the stream and proceeded to do what looked like hula dance movements. This allowed logs to ricochet off their rumps, with force, into the center of the quickly flowing water! There was not one log that damaged the piers. The crowd cheered and once again, the magnificence of intellect, strength, and determination of the elephant was provided. (Croke, 2015)[3].

Lesson

This is a powerful story of a community banding together to save people and enrich the lives of others. There was no big exchange of money, but there was a combination of knowledge, creativity, impressive animal strength, and people united to save villages downstream. Having people come together to help one another is a key factor for strengthening community and country. Social unrest and turbulence are part of history, however, to select violence over seeking peaceful solutions to real problems is the pathway to increased bigotry and prejudice. As one person responds instead of reacting to taunts, they teach others to do so as well. When a neighbor offers kindness and service to another, they model behavior which embraces the tenets of the Golden Rule, "Do Unto Others as Others Would Have Them Do Unto You."

Do joy and happiness fall from a tree? Is it an end-product or can you find happiness on the journey through life? With this community bonding together, there was a lot of happiness and satisfaction, excited anticipation as villagers witnessed the work of the elephants and the results of those efforts. Happiness is abstract, it is part of the journey, it often comes only when we search for meaning in a moment and it comes at the embrace of a loved one. And, very importantly, it comes in recognizing one's potentials and actualizing those. Williams knew how to actualize the potential in the elephants and the community. He was a role model and leader.

Each of us is born with tremendous gifts. Some are in mathematics, logic, science, research, analysis. Others in dreaming of what can be, visual arts, aesthetics, and some in being incredibly sensitive to others and having a foundation of patience, integrity, and kindness. And, each of us has a combination of these. When one lives in harmony with self, they are more likely to experience frequent happiness.

There is a term in psychology, subjective well-being. How would you rate yours right this very minute that you are reading this? Stop, sit back, take a slow breath in, and ask yourself, "How would I define my own well-being? How would I rate it?"

Can we find happiness amidst our challenges? Of course! Can we find joy in the moment? Definitely. When a child smiles there is immediate joy. When you are recognized and acknowledged just for being a fellow human being there is a sense of belonging. When one tunes into the moment and focuses attention on gratitude there can be joy, peace, and awareness of a deeper appreciation for life.

In this very hectic world where animosity abounds, is it possible that each of us can be the conduit to happiness? Can I be that bridge of strength to lead others to hope?

Activity:

1. You have 60 seconds to draw as many emoticons as you can.
2. Now, count how many are positive and happy.
3. How many are sad and angry?
4. Design 10 new designs you could call emoticons or anything you want.
5. Each student holds up one of their new designs and the others guess what it means. ENJOY!

Footnote

1   Croke, V. C. (2015, April). The day the elephants danced. Readers Digest. Found online October 29, 2020 from https://vickicroke.com/.

2   Ibid.

3   Ibid.

Lesson 38

The Mantle of Mentorship

Success is not how high you have climbed,
but how you make a positive difference to the world.
- Roy T. Bennett, <u>The Light in the Heart</u>

Clearing Debris

It was a beautiful town in the Austrian mountains. A stream ran through it, bringing water and beauty. In the nearby forest lived a man who kept to himself. For years he had been hired to keep the stream clear of debris. Higher up the mountain pools of water would collect, then leaves, rocks, branches and other debris would fall into it. The gentleman of the forest had one job, to keep the pools cleared and the stream clean. This resulted in a booming economy for the little village. It was so beautiful that it soon became a tourist attraction. The water accumulated into a beautiful spot of refuge. The farms were irrigated, the town provided clean water, and the tourists enjoyed the ambience of the village. Swans gracefully floated over the lake. The mill wheels churned night and day.

Several years passed and some new members were added to the city council. One questioned the salary allotted to the lone forest man, even questioning why he was getting paid and suggesting that perhaps he was not doing anything but receiving a check. The committee agreed and cut the budget and the man was fired.

Initially, nothing changed, but after a few weeks the stream showed a different color, it wasn't as clear, there was a yellowish-brown tint. Branches fell into the pools of water higher upstream and clogged the water. The mill wheels turned more slowly then finally stopped. Disease and sickness came from the water to the villagers. Suddenly the council realized their grave mistake and immediately hired the quiet man again to keep the stream clear. Within a few days the mill wheels churned to life and the water was filtered through once again showing a beautiful, pristine stream. The power of this one man to make a difference was immense. Without his work the production stopped, and people got sick. With his daily efforts, crops were nourished, the villagers cared for, and businesses flourished. (Lirez, 2010)[1].

Lesson

This is the story of one man making a difference. It is also a story of others who neglected to research into the why of a situation to fully assess possible consequences. Little things matter. Each day one step in any direction guides your compass. Where do you want your compass focused? What do you want for yourself and others? How can you be the Man Upstream to bring wisdom, knowledge, better health and hope to others?

This course is designed for you, to help you become your greatest self. A key component is service, but in doing so, always try to ask how you can provide the greatest service to others. How can you become a great mentor throughout the remainder of your life? A mentor is someone you can rely on and trust. They have your best interests at heart, and they provide a foundation of safety and reliability. Often, they provide the light you may need to help you get through a particular season of life. This applies to you helping others.

Return to the picture at the beginning of this lesson. There are several things to notice. The most obvious is the sunset. This picture is from a collection I took as I watched the effects of wildfires in the far distance with the resultant aura around the sun. A mentor provides a light. They offer hope and direction. But what are other things you notice? There are several large branches that have broken off and fallen, but the area surrounding them is filled with greenery. This is growth, this is beauty, and this is symbolic of the power within each person to rise up and move forward in life. You may get knocked down, but many people around you are there to provide the nutrients to help pull you up to try again.

Activity

This lesson presents a series of questions inviting you to reflect upon your own integrity, interests, and readiness for the opportunity to mentor others. Where would you be if you felt no one cared? If you feel that way now, what can make the difference for you? These are questions to consider as you learn from mistakes made and make new choices for each tomorrow.

1. Draw a tree. Include many branches.
2. On each branch in bold print write a quality or characteristic you want to bring to others as a mentor. Some ideas are honesty, trust, patience, kindness.
3. Now draw a ladder to each branch. On the ladder write topics you feel you can help people with, for instance, reading, math, writing, art, music.
4. Now, sketch penetrating, strong roots for your tree. This is to provide a visual of a strong foundation within yourself and for you to realize you can offer others.

Footnotes

1   Lirez, M (2010). The 100 top inspirational anecdotes and stores. (Offered through Kindle Deluxe, location 1123 in the book).

Lesson 39

Wearing the Armor of Integrity and Kindness

Picture courtesy of mysticartsdesign found on
https://pixabay.com/illustrations/
gladiator-rome-roman-history-fight-1771625/

Rise to the challenge and become the captain of your own
thoughts, beliefs, decisions and actions. Have faith in God. Walk
with courage and keep your positive mental imagination alive.
Whenever you fall, waste no time in getting back up. It is only a
matter of time until something miraculous happens in your life.
— **Edmond Mbiaka**

The Grinch

You choose to succeed. You can see where any armor of self-sabotaging
behaviors has not empowered you on your course through life. You have

realized your strengths and now you want to mentor others. You have a clearer view of your goals and your potential. To understand success, we need to also realize the importance of healthy relationships. We need to learn how to design stronger bridges of communication with one another, and we need to be able to look beyond the obvious and see the story beneath the "storm" when someone is angry and resentful. Consider the movie "How the Grinch Stole Christmas" which originated with the book. In it we meet a very mean, and quite humorous grinch. But what is a grinch? Merriam-Webster defines one as "…a grumpy person who spoils the pleasure of others." (https://www.merriam-webster.com/dictionary/grinch (Links to an external site.)

This grinch was certainly mean and vindictive. He was obsessed with destroying Christmas. He lived in Whoville, a village where the people seemed kind and generous. But this Grinch was angry. He had stomped around for fifty-three years and grumbled about Christmas, yes, for fifty-three years he held a grudge. So, one year he designed an intricate plan of destruction and had great joy through enacting it. He snuck into Whoville and stole the presents, the food, Christmas stockings, anything that anyone would equate with the Christmas season.

(Picture courtesy of Kerbstone @pixabay.
https://pixabay.com/illustrations/
grinch-xmas-christmas-santa-humour-1038238/)

Where people thought there was no hope for this "Grinch" person, a child saw a spark within his soul. Through her kindness that spark finally grew into a flame, one which brought joy to others. Yes, just as the Grinch was ready to celebrate his naughtiness, he stopped and considered his actions. He thought about the little girl's words and kindness, and then he realized something which totally amazed him. The people did not care about the presents, they only thought about the love and concern they had for one another. What? How could this be, and what was that radiance they shared with each other? (Khurana, 2020)[1].

Dr. Seuss was a master at intertwining lessons
for life through his delightful prose.

And the Grinch, with his grinch-feet ice-cold in the snow,
Stood puzzling and puzzling: 'How could it be so?'
It came without ribbons! It came without tags!
It came without packages, boxes or bags!
And he puzzled three hours, till his puzzler was sore.
Then the Grinch thought of something he hadn't before!
'Maybe Christmas,' he thought, 'doesn't come from a store.

-Dr. Seuss

Look at the last line, "Maybe Christmas doesn't come from a store." What a thought! Regardless of one's religious affiliation, for millions of people Christmas is known to be a season of joy and giving. The Christian celebrates the birth of the Savior, Jesus Christ. Others may view it simply as the time for Santa, presents, and celebration.

Let us compare this to family and friends, those who love us for who we are and nurture us when life feels like a storm of epic proportions. The Grinch was a wounded soul. He was cruel because he was rejected and felt abandoned. He was lonely and sad yet could not face his true emotions, so he projected his anger onto others. Then, through the gentleness of a smile, a word from a child, he turned his anger around. He realized that the meaning of Christmas or any holiday is not about presents, those are fun trimmings, but the true meaning is in the bonding of relationships and love shared between people, learning to forgive, and walking in the pathway of peace. He released his armor of anger and embraced a heart of charity, compassion, and generosity.

This course is designed to invite great introspection on your part to know at a more profound level who you are and how powerful your influence on others is and can continue to be.

Most people going into battle will have some sort of armor. Sometimes life can be a battle. The Grinch used negative armor tactical to protect his wounded heart. He ruminated, meaning that he continually rehearsed all the pain he had received from others, he fed his anger at the citizens of Whoville, and he engaged in devious planning to ruin Christmas by stealing all that he perceived to be their greatest prizes.

Let us now consider spiritual armor. This is the ability to talk through things rather than hoard them like candy, which causes the decay of the soul. Spiritual armor invites self and others to stop, breathe slowly, remain calm, and use words and kindness rather than violence. The question is, how can YOU put on an armor of being a good person who truly makes a difference? Regardless of your spirituality or religion, the words in Ephesians are powerful for every person to consider.

Lesson: Ephesians 6:11-17 states:

11 Put on the whole armour of God, that ye may be able to stand against the wiles of the devil.

12 For we wrestle not against flesh and blood, but against principalities, against powers, against the rulers of the darkness of this world, against spiritual wickedness in high places.

13 Wherefore take unto you the whole armour of God, that ye may be able to withstand in the evil day, and having done all, to stand.

14 Stand therefore, having your loins girt about with truth, and having on the breastplate of righteousness;

15 And your feet shod with the preparation of the gospel of peace;

16 Above all, taking the shield of faith, wherewith ye shall be able to quench all the fiery darts of the wicked.

17 And take the helmet of salvation, and the sword of the Spirit, which is the word of God:

18 Praying always with all prayer and supplication in the Spirit, and watching thereunto with all perseverance and supplication for all saints;

Breaking this down into modern day terms we have the following:

1. (Verse 11): When you are focused on God you are able to overcome temptation, heal from pain and addiction, and move forward with courage.
2. (Verse 12): Your wrestle is not with man but with your own soul. Which do you choose, God or Satan? The first will free you, the second will imprison you internally and often, externally. The first offers strength in principle and values, the second offers false promises that will, indeed, prove your downfall.
3. (Verse 13): Total commitment to God, to being a righteous, kind person, a law-abiding person who helps others.
4. (Verse 14): Total commitment to truth and to doing what is right in any given situation.
5. (Verse 15): Be one who brings peace, who speaks in peaceful terms, who invites peace, not conflict.
6. (Verse 16); This invites you to be a person with faith that things will get better.
7. (Verse 17): Be a person who learns the word of God and has it as his/her foundation. This includes the Ten Commandments.
8. (Verse 18) Be a person of prayer and silent reflection. Pray for yourself, your family, friends, and all others. Pray to be a man/woman of high character and compassion.

Activity:

1. Draw a shield of armor for yourself.
2. Write meaningful words or draw symbols to represent how you view your own armor. Consider your choice of colors and the words of honor you will include.

3. As a mentor what principles or values do you want to teach those you will work with?

Footnote

1   Khurana, Simran. (2020, February 11). Moral Lessons From 'How the Grinch Stole Christmas'. Retrieved from https://www.thoughtco.com/important-lesson-about-christmas-from-grinch-2831927

Lesson 40

Moving Forward with Clarity

*Life is like riding a bicycle, to keep your
balance, you must keep moving.*
-Albert Einstein

Congratulations on your commitment to this course that was designed towards increased awareness of one's self-efficacy. The course provides tutelage for becoming a mentor and leader to guide others towards the fulfillment of their dreams and goals. You can now move forward with more clarity. In Dr. Dan Seligman's (2006) book, *Learned Optimism,* he promoted the attitude of "I can" rather than the pessimism and helplessness of "I can't." He showed the association between thoughts and health and the importance of changing personal beliefs from negativism to optimism.[1] This is the new you, the optimistic, confident, yet humble you.

Remember, YOU have the power within to succeed in the accomplishments of your goals. You can make a positive difference in the lives of everyone you meet. It is YOUR choice. As you cast diamonds of knowledge, insight, compassion, and empathy you are making the world a better place. As you mentor with patience, direction, and positivity you have offered new possibilities to others who are struggling. The rest is up to them to learn from you, their mentor, and seek after their own acres of joy.

You have completed an important course, a major stepping-stone in your work towards become an emotionally savvy adult. After taking the inventory you will receive a certificate of completion. I thank you for your work in completing this course.

Footnote

1   Seligman, D. (2006). Learned helplessness. NY, NY: Random House.

Booth Self- Assessment Inventory

Instructions: Rate each item using a scale of
1 to 5 then answer the question.

1 Strongly Disagree, 2 = Disagree, 3 = Neutral, 4 = Agree, 5 = Strongly Agree

1. I choose to be honest in my dealings.

   1 Strongly Disagree 2 Disagree 3 Unsure 4 Agree 5 Strongly Agree

   What does this mean to you?

2. I find it important to make sure my behaviors are in line with my beliefs.

   1 Strongly Disagree 2 Disagree 3 Unsure 4 Agree 5 Strongly Agree

   Comments: Clarify your beliefs by completing the statements. Some ideas are being honest, being loyal, dependable, kind, true to my word, moral, empathetic, having hope, helping others, etc…

   I believe in …

   I believe in …

   I believe in …

   I believe in …

   I believe in…

3. In the past I followed the crowd, even if I knew what they were doing was wrong.

   1 Strongly Disagree 2 Disagree 3 Unsure 4 Agree 5 Strongly Agree

   Describe your feelings now; looking back on the "previous" you, compared to the present, how have you changed you?

4. I believe in myself.

   1 Strongly Disagree 2 Disagree 3 Unsure 4 Agree 5 Strongly Agree

   Describing what believing in yourself means to you.

5. I can accomplish my goals.

   1 Strongly Disagree 2 Disagree 3 Unsure 4 Agree 5 Strongly Agree

   Describe what you believe you can accomplish.

6. When I don't act in line with my beliefs, I feel remorse.

   1 Strongly Disagree 2 Disagree 3 Unsure 4 Agree 5 Strongly Agree

   Provide an example of not acting in line with your beliefs.

7. There are some people I believe have my bests interests in mind.

   1 Strongly Disagree 2 Disagree 3 Unsure 4 Agree 5 Strongly Agree

   List these people and how they show you that they care and want you to experience.

8. There are ways I show that I am honest.

   1 Strongly Disagree 2 Disagree 3 Unsure 4 Agree 5 Strongly Agree

   List three ways you prove that you are honest.

9. I consider other's feelings when I say or plan to do something.

1 Strongly Disagree 2 Disagree 3 Unsure 4 Agree 5 Strongly Agree

Comments: Explain with an example.

10. I am resistant to change.

1   2   3   4   5   6   7   8   9   10

Comments: Are you open to learning new ways of doing things and to use those ideas? Provide an example.

11. No matter how hard I try I never succeed.

1 Strongly Disagree 2 Disagree 3 Unsure 4 Agree 5 Strongly Agree

Provide an example.

12. I am willing to do what it takes to change and make a better life for myself, a life without harming others.

1 Strongly Disagree 2 Disagree 3 Unsure 4 Agree 5 Strongly Agree

What do you view as your biggest obstacle in changing?

13. It is up to me to make a success of myself.

1 Strongly Disagree 2 Disagree 3 Unsure 4 Agree 5 Strongly Agree

If you answered that you agree, when did you realize this?

14. I am clear in my goals for what I want to accomplish in the next twelve months.

1 Strongly Disagree 2 Disagree 3 Unsure 4 Agree 5 Strongly Agree

What is your one-year goal?

15. I am clear in my goals for what I want to accomplish in the next five years.

   1 Strongly Disagree 2 Disagree 3 Unsure 4 Agree 5 Strongly Agree

   What are your five-year goals?

16. I would like to be trained as a youth mentor.

   1 Strongly Disagree 2 Disagree 3 Unsure 4 Agree 5 Strongly Agree

   Describe how you see yourself helping others.

17. I know where I would like to do an internship.

   1 Strongly Disagree 2 Disagree 3 Unsure 4 Agree 5 Strongly Agree

   Describe your desired internship.

18. Describe one to three areas you feel you could mentor youth.

REFERENCES

Ackerman, C. E. (2019, Nov 7). Big Five Personality Traits: The OCEAN Model Explained.

Retrieved 17 December 2019 from https://positivepsychology.com/big-five-personality-theory/

Alcoholics Anonymous. History of Alcoholics Anonymous). (en.wikipedia.org/wiki/History_of_Alcoholics_Anonymous

Anne Frank http://www.biography.com/people/anne-frank-9300892#nazi-occupation

Andrews, A. (2002). *The Traveler's Gift*. Nashville, TE. W. Publishing Group.

Bhasin, H. (2019, Dec 2). What is the importance of learning (In any stage of life). https://www.marketing91.com/importance-of-learning/

Bariso, J. (2018). EQ Applied: The Real World Guide to Emotional Intelligence. Germany: Borough Hall.

Basinger, R. (2020, May). Odette samson: The most decorated woman of world war II. https://www.identifymedals.com/article/odette-sansom-the-most-decorated-woman-of-world-war-ii/ I.

Biography.com Editors. (2019, Aug 20). Louis Zamperini biography.

Bozic, N., Lawthom, R., and Murray, J. (2018), Exploring the context of strengths – a new approach to strength-based assessment. *Educational Psychology in Practice*. Vol 34 No.

"Candy Bomber Delivered Chocolate, Hope to Berlin." (14 September 2018). *Airman Magazine*.

Cowley, M. (1953, May 18). Achievement. https://speeches.byu.edu/talks/matthew-cowley/achievement/

Covey, S. (2004). The 7 habits of highly effective people: Powerful lessons in personal change. NY: Simon & Schuster.

Craig, H. (2019, Jan 8). 17 Emotional intelligence tests and assessments. Positivepsychology.com Retrieved from https://positivepsychology.com/emotional-intelligence-tests/

Croke, V. C. (2015, April). The day the elephants danced. Readers Digest. Found online October 29, 2020 from https://vickicroke.com/.

Curran, L. A. (2010) *Trauma Competency. A Clinician's Guide*. PESI: Eau Claire, WI.

Davis, A. & Harrigan, J. R. (2019, Sept 6). The Cobra Effect: Lessons in Unintended Consequences. *Foundation for Economic Education*. Retrieved from https://fee.org/articles/the-cobra-effect-lessons-in-unintended-consequences/

Dispenza, J. (2014, May 23). How I Healed Myself After Breaking 6 Vertebrae: The Placebo Effect in Action. *You Can Heal Your Life*. Retrieved (18 December 2019) from https://www.healyourlife.com/how-i-healed-myself-after-breaking-6-vertebrae

Dispenza, J. & McNay, L. (n.d.) 'The Science of Changing Your Mind'. Retrieved (18 December 2019) from https://video.search.yahoo.com/search/video?fr=mcafee&p=the+science+of+change+with+joe+dispenza#id=5&vid=8ce7a0324fde9ae0f8896156cbc6e22a&action=view.

Fadiman, C. (Ed.). (1985). *The Little Brown Book of Anecdotes*. NY: Hachette Book Group. P. 339

Frank, Otto. (1952). *Anne frank: Diary of a young girl*. New York, NY: Bantam Books.

Freedman, J. (2005, Jan 30). Dr. daniel goleman on the origins of emotional intelligence. *Six seconds*.

George Washington Carver Facts for Kids. *Kiddle Encyclopedia*. Found online (16 December 2019) from https://kids.kiddle.co/George_Washington_Carver

Gluck, Keith. (2011, Nov 18). The Birth of a Mouse. *The Walt Disney Family Museum (2018)*. Retrieved from https://www.waltdisney.org/blog/birth-mouse

Goleman, D. (1998). *Working with Emotional Intelligence*. NY: Bantom Dell.

Greenberg, M. (2012, Oct 1). The 50 Best Quotes on Self-Love. Found online December 17, 2019 from https://www.psychologytoday.com/us/blog/the-mindful-self-express/201210/the-50-best-quotes-self-love

Harrington Rod Definition. Spine Health. https://www.spine-health.com/glossary/harringtonrod

Hillenbrand, L. (2010). *Unbroken*. NY: Random House.

History.Com Editors. (2020, Jul 1) *Anne frank*. https://www.history.com/topics/world-war-ii/annefrank-1

History.com Editors. (2009, Dec 18). The SS. https.//www.history.com/
topics/world-warii/ss.

John, O. P., & Srivastava, S. (1999). The Big-Five trait taxonomy: History,
measurement, and theoretical perspectives. In L. A. Pervin & O. P.
John (Eds.), *Handbook of Personality: Theory and Research* (Vol. 2, pp.
102-138). New York: Guilford Press.

Khurana, Simran. (2020, February 11). Moral Lessons From 'How
the Grinch Stole Christmas. https://www.thoughtco.com/
important-lesson-about-christmas-from-grinch-2831927

Konikova, M. (2014, Oct 9). The Struggles of a Psychologist Studying
Self-Control. *New Yorker.*

Lad, K. (2019, Mar 26). Undeniably Interesting Facts about Walt
Disney's Childhood. Retrieved from https://entertainism.com/
walt-disneys-childhood

Lebowitz, S. (2016a). The 'Big 5' personality traits could
predict who will and won't become a leader. *Business
Insider.* Retrieved from http://www.businessinsider.com/
big-five-personality-traits-predict-leadership-2016-12

Lirez, M (2010). The 100 top inspirational anecdotes and stores. (Offered
through Kindle Deluxe).

Mahatma gandhi biography. (2018, Mar 1). *Biography Online.* Retrieved
from https://www.biographyonline.net/politicians/indian/gandhi.html

Martin Luther King. (2020, January 14). *Biography.* https://www.
biography.com/activist/martin-luther-king-jr

Mayer, J. D., Salovey, P., & Caruso, D. (2004). Emotional intelligence:
theory, findings, and implications. *Psychological Inquiry*, 15, 197–215

Michael Dowling, Most Inspiring Figure. A Ford on a Lincoln. Found
online August 10, 2020 @ https://llafordonthelincoln.blogspot.
com/2017/07/45- michael-dowling-mostinspiringfigure.html

MLB Network (Producers) (2016, July 10). The bird. *MLB Network.*
*Mohandes gandhi marries kasturbai makhanji in an arranged child
marriage.* (2020). *World history project. The history of us.* Retrieved from
https://worldhistoryproject.org/1883/5/mohandes-gandhi-marries-
kasturbai-makhanji-in-an-arranged-child-marriage

Moore, T. (2004). Dark nights of the soul. NY: Penguin Publishing Group.
Kindle Edition.

Nolasco, S. (2020, Jan 4). Former teen idol Leif Garrett explains descent into hard drugs: 'There has always been more to my story.' *Fox News*. Retrieved from https://www.foxnews.com/entertainment/leif-garrett-teen-idol-memoir

Odette Sansom Biography (n.d.) taken from Odette Hallowes, *The Times*. (17 March 1975). Found online 12/22/19 retrieved https://www.biographyonline.net/military/odette-sanson.html

O'Leary, J. (2016). *On fire: The 7 choices to ignite a radically inspired life.* NY: Gallery Books.

Pettinger, T. (2011). Biography of mahatma gandhi. Oxford, UK. *www.biographyonline.net* 12th Jan 2011. Last updated 1 March 2018.

Pitogo, H. (2015, March 30). WWII Stories: Odette Sansom, the First Woman to Receive the George Cross. War History Online. Retrieved from https://www.warhistoryonline.com/war-articles/wwii-stories-odette-sansom-the-firstwoman-to-receive-the-george-cross.html

Pro Edit. (2013). Understanding bloom's (and anderson and krathwohl's) taxonomy. (2013). from https://www.proedit.com/understanding-blooms-and-anderson-and-krathwohls-taxonomy/

Schutte, N. S., Malouff, J. M. Thorsteinsson, E. B. Bhullar, N., and Rooke, S. E. (11 October 2006). A meta-analytic investigation of the relationship between emotional intelligence and health Personality and Individual Differences 42 (2007) 921–933. Retrieved from ScienceDirect.com(https://www.researchgate.net/profile/Einar_Thorsteinsson/publication/216626194_A_metaanalytic_investigation_of_the_relationship_between_emotional_intelligence_and_health/links/5b1793...) February 26, 2020.

Schutte, N. S., Malouff, J. M., Simunek, M., Hollander, S., & McKenley, J. (2002). Characteristic emotional intelligence and emotional well-being. Cognition and Emotion, 16, 769–786.

Seligman, M. E. P. (2006). Learned optimism. New York, NY: Random House.

Sharma, D., Mishra, I. and Sharma, M.V. (2014). Emotional intelligence among employees of government and public sectors. *International Journal of Social Sciences. Vol. 3 (3).*

Sharma, S. (2017, Nov 17). The boy and the drum. *Bedtime short stories*. Retrieved from https://www.bedtimeshortstories.com/the-boy-and-the-drum

Soldz, S., & Vaillant, G. E. (1999). The Big Five personality traits and the life course: A 45-year longitudinal study. *Journal of Research in Personality, 33,* 208-232. doi:10.1006/jrpe.1999.2243

Spiegel, R. (2020). 46 magical facts about walt Disney. https://www.factinate.com/people/46-magical-facts-walt Disney/#:~:text=Walt%Disney%20 Facts.

Stevens, K. (2009). *Where the Blind Horse Sings* [Kindle E-reader version]. NY: Sky Horse Publishing. Retrieved from https://www.amazon.com/gp/product/160239055X?pf_rd_p=ab873d20-a0ca-439b-ac45-cd78f07a84d8&pf_rd_r=VAW69F29HFXFB1G4CJVC

Tasker, Roy. (2016). Upside Down & Backwards with the Law of Attraction. Avatar Publications, Inc.

Ten Boom, C. (2006). *The Hiding Place*. Grand Rapids, MI: Chosen Books.

The Fence. (2010, Nov 7). TEACHNET.COM Retrieved from http://teachnet.com/communicate/inspiration/story-the-fence/

Verger, R. (2019, July 18). The apollo 11 mission as told through the astronaut's heartrate. *Popular science.*

Watson, C. (2018). *The language of kindness.* NY: Duggan Books.

Williams, M. (nd) *The velveteen rabbit.* [E-reader version]. NY: Open Road Integrated Media. Retrieved from smile.amazon.com.

Printed in the United States
By Bookmasters